MONTANA
TRIVIA

JANET SPENCER

Trivia queen
I am!

RIVERBEND
PUBLISHING

Copyright © 2005 by Janet Spencer

Published by Riverbend Publishing, Helena, Montana.

Printed in the United States of America.

6 7 8 9 0 MG 10 09 08 07

Cover design by Bob Smith
Text design by Suzan Glosser

ISBN 1-931832-60-9

Cataloging-in-Publication data is on file at the Library of Congress.

Riverbend Publishing
P.O. Box 5833
Helena, MT 59604
1-866-787-2363
www.riverbendpublishing.com

Contents

BOOKS BY JANET SPENCER

MONTANA TRIVIA
THE TIDBITS TREASURY OF TRIVIA AND COMPENDIUM OF MISCELLANY

CONTRIBUTOR TO UNCLE JOHN'S BATHROOM READERS:
THE AHH-INSPIRING BATHROOM READER
THE SUPREMELY SATISFYING BATHROOM READER
THE UNSTOPPABLE BATHROOM READER
THE BATHROOM READER FOR KIDS

ACKNOWLEDGMENTS

From the time I first experienced the magic of Montana, I wanted to write books about the state. I'm so happy to have the chance to do so. Montana is a miraculous place and it gives me great joy to share some of that with others.

Many people played a part in the creation of this book. Particularly helpful were the people who, on numerous occasions, answered their phone to find it was me (again) with yet *another* question. Among them were Sara, Diana, and the staff at Lewis and Clark County Library (the oldest library in the state—see the Arts & Literature chapter); the staff at the Census & Economic Information Center as well as the Montana Historical Society (which was formed only seven months after Montana was declared a territory—see the History chapter); George Everett, who knows more about Butte than anyone else on earth (see *all* chapters); Kathleen Ely for sharing her vast knowledge of Montana literature; Marie McAlear for loading me up with county trivia; Patti and Bill Borneman for numerous trivial tips; Guido Bugni for all those fascinating file folders from the bottomless basement; Vic Richer for internet research; Vic Reiman for heaps of help; and Vince ("Who's the best proofreader in Montana?") Moravek for saving me from many potential embarrassments. Also Mrs. Story, my 5th grade teacher, for telling me I should become a writer when I grew up, which I did.

Special warm and fuzzy springtime-in-Montana gratitude to my husband Jerry for bringing me to Montana in the first place, and for keeping me fed while I wrote this book; and my parents, Dr. Hal and Edie Malehorn, especially since my dad taught me by example how wonderful it is to write books.

GEOGRAPHY

Q. What do you call a person from Montana?
- ♦ a Montanidian
- ♦ a Montanoid
- ♦ a Montanian
- ♦ a Montanonian
- ♦ a Montanite
- ♦ a Montanan
- ♦ a Montaner

A. A Montanan.

Q. How many states have a larger land area than Montana's 147,046 square miles?
A. Three: Alaska, California, and Texas.

Q. Is the 550-mile east-to-west distance from one end of Montana to the other greater than, less than, or equal to the distance from Chicago to New York City?
A. About equal to, as the crow flies.

Q. "Montana" comes from the Latin and Spanish word for what?
A. Mountainous.

Q. Where can you find some of the oldest rocks on earth, estimated to be between three and four billion years old?
A. In Glacier National Park, where the Lewis Overthrust Fault piled old rocks on top of new.

Q. A volcanic explosion in Yellowstone two million years ago was how large, when compared to Mount St. Helens?
A. 2,500 times bigger than the Mount St. Helens blast.

Q. A laccolith, formed when a blister of magma rises but cannot break through to the surface and hardens, later to be revealed by erosion, is sometimes known by what common name?
A. A butte, such as Round Butte, Square Butte, and Crown Butte near Great Falls.

Q. Where does Montana reach its lowest altitude of 1,889 feet?
A. In the northwestern corner, where the Kootenai River enters Idaho.

Q. Montana's highest elevation of 12,799 feet is found at what place?
A. Granite Peak in the Beartooth Mountains.

Q. Where would you find the third largest single expanse of land above 10,000 feet in elevation in the lower 48 states?
A. In the Absaroka-Beartooth Wilderness. Only California's Sierra Nevada and Wyoming's Wind River Range are higher.

Q. How many of the 50 highest points in the state are located in the Beartooth Range near Yellowstone?
A. All of them. It's the only range in the state with peaks over 12,000 feet.

Q. What mountain range qualifies as Montana's second highest range?
A. The Madison Range, which runs from Yellowstone to Bozeman. There are 75 peaks over 11,000 feet in the Beartooths but only six in the Madison Range.

Q. Forming the western border, what is the longest mountain range in the state?
A. The Bitterroots, just over 200 miles long.

Q. When a million prehistoric grasshoppers of a now-extinct species got caught in a storm and died of the cold, they landed on a glacier where they are now embedded in ice in what mountain range?
A. Grasshopper Glacier is in the Beartooth Mountains, at 11,000 feet.

Q. Montana is the fourth most geologically active state, behind what other three?
A. Alaska, California, and Hawaii.

Q. How many earthquakes rattled Helena in the fall and winter of 1935, including two that caused widespread damage and killed four people?
A. More than 1,200, including one of magnitude 6.3 and another of 6.0.

Q. Which is Montana's most seismically active county, on a par with the San Andreas Fault in California?
A. Madison County, just northwest of Yellowstone.

Q. When a magnitude 7.5 quake hit the Yellowstone area in 1959, causing an entire mountainside to crash into the Madison River and burying a campground under tons of rock, how many people were killed?
A. 28, 19 of whose bodies have never been recovered.

Q. When that landslide blocked the flow of the Madison River, what new lake was formed?
A. Quake Lake, where the skeletons of drowned trees still poke above the surface.

Q. With its headwaters in Montana, what is the nation's longest river?
A. The Missouri, which is 2,540 miles long (200 miles longer than the Mississippi).

Q. Why did the Missouri River, which formerly drained into Hudson Bay, change its course?
A. Ice age glaciers blocked its path and its current course now follows the ancient glacial front.

Q. Listed by the Guinness Book of World Records as the world's shortest river, how long is the Roe River as it flows from Giant Springs to the Missouri River near Great Falls?
A. 201 feet.

Q. Giant Springs, one of the largest freshwater springs in the world, pumps out how many gallons of water per hour?
A. 7.9 million, at a constant temperature of 54 degrees Fahrenheit, carbon dated at 3,000 years old.

Q. From the source of a river to the point where it exits the state, what is the average descent in altitude for a typical Montana river?
A. 3,000 feet.

Q. What peak in Glacier National Park is the only place in the world whose rivers reach three different seas: The Gulf of Mexico, the Arctic Ocean, and the Pacific Ocean?
A. Triple Divide Peak.

Q. How many Indian reservations are there in the state?
A. Seven, covering some 13,055 square miles, about nine percent of Montana land.

Q. What percentage of the land in the United States still belongs to Indian nations?
A. Four percent.

Q. What Indian reservation was supposed to be named after Chief Stone Child, but was mistranslated from Chippewa into English?
A. Rocky Boy's.

Q. Compared to the three cents per acre that President Thomas Jefferson paid the French for the Louisiana Purchase in 1803, what is the price per acre of average Montana cropland today?
A. $540. North Dakota is the only state with cheaper land; New Jersey is the most expensive at $9,990 per acre.

Q. How long did it take Lewis and Clark to portage the 18 miles around the five waterfalls of Great Falls?
A. 32 days.

Q. Why is Great Falls called the Electric City?
A. Because there are five hydroelectric dams on the Missouri River, largely obscuring the great falls.

Q. What percentage of the Lewis and Clark expedition took place inside the modern-day boundaries of Montana?
A. About 25 percent, more than any other state.

Q. Which member of the Lewis and Clark expedition carved his name in the rock of Pompey's Pillar in 1806, leaving the only physical evidence of their passing?
A. William Clark.

Q. The Judith River was named after Judith Hancock, William Clark's cousin whom he was infatuated with and later married; how old was she when he named the river after her?
A. 13. They had five children together.

Q. When officials in Idaho Territory agreed to cede some land to form the new state of Montana, where did they expect the boundary would be drawn?
A. The Continental Divide. Political shenanigans resulted in the boundary being the Bitterroot Mountains instead, leaving Idaho a strange panhandle.

Q. In a treaty with England in 1846, what parallel of latitude became Montana's—and America's—northern boundary?
A. 49th.

Q. Where was the first major gold strike in Montana on July 29, 1862?
A. Grasshopper Creek, resulting in the city of Bannack, the first territorial capital.

Q. The town of Bannack, Montana's first town with a population of 500 in 1862, officially changed its name to what in 1864 when the population reached 1,000?
A. Bannack City.

Q. What town had some 50 millionaires in the 1880s, which was more millionaires per capita than any other community in the nation?
A. Helena.

Q. What was proposed (and voted down) in the 1920s to correct the common mispronunciation of Helena as Hel-EEN-a?
A. Changing the spelling to Hellena.

Q. What town, located as far inland as a person could possibly navigate by boat on any continent without portaging, became known as the "world's innermost port"?
A. Fort Benton, some 3,560 miles from the Gulf of Mexico.

Q. The state penitentiary today is in what town, which was the site of the first territorial prison?
A. Deer Lodge.

Q. What county now has the greatest ratio of men to women, with 139 males to every 100 women?
A. Powell, with Deer Lodge as the county seat. An average of 1,440 men reside at the State Penitentiary there.

Q. Are there more prisoners or law enforcement officers in the state?
A. There are about 2,200 people in prison and only 1,760 officers.

Q. When Montana was declared a state in 1889, what percentage of the residents had been born in the state?
A. 15 percent.

Q. In the 2000 Census, what percentage of people living in the state were born there?
A. 57 percent, compared to 70 percent in Utah (the most) and 15 percent in Nevada (the least).

Q. What is the current population of Montana?
A. 926,865 as of July 2004, which is about how many people live in the city of Detroit.

Q. What Montana city had the largest population in 1917, making it the biggest city between Minneapolis and Seattle?
A. Butte, with around 90,000 people.

Q. What is the population of the Butte area today?
A. 33,892.

Q. The census taken during what year was the first to show that more Montanans were living in cities than in rural areas in the state?
A. 1960.

Q. What percentage of Montana residents currently live in rural areas?
A. 48 percent, compared to a national average of 25 percent.

Q. When a mining engineer named Mr. Deidensheimer built a stamp mill, a new town grew around it. Residents were determined to name the city after him, but chose his first name rather than his last. What town is it?
A. Philipsburg.

Q. How many ghost towns are there across the state?
A. More than 60.

Q. In what town would you find the Ghost Town Hall of Fame?
A. Philipsburg, in Granite County.

Q. How many communities populated Granite County in 1900?
A. 18, with a total county population of 4,328.

Q. How many communities populate Granite County today?
A. Four, with a total county population of 2,830.

Q. What was the only decade in the state's history to experience a net population drop?
A. The 1920s, because of drought— the only state in the United States to lose population that decade.

Q. In the 1920s when Montana's rate of tax foreclosure ranked second in the nation, what was the only state with more foreclosures?
A. Mississippi.

Q. Between 1921 and 1925, what percentage of Montana farmers lost their homesteads to mortgage foreclosure?
A. 50 percent.

Q. In what year was the highest rate of suicides recorded in the state?
A. 1930, when 25 out of every 100,000 residents committed suicide.

Q. Montana has 56 counties now, but how many were there right after Montana was declared a state in 1889?
A. Only nine really large ones.

Q. Which of Montana's 56 counties is the largest, equal to the states of Connecticut and Rhode Island combined?
A. Beaverhead County with 5,542 square miles, is the 40th largest county in the U.S. (San Bernardino County, east of L.A., is the biggest at 20,160 square miles.)

Q. Which is the smallest county?
A. Silver Bow with Butte as the county seat has 714 square miles, a little more than half the size of Rhode Island.

Q. What county is 80 percent Indian reservation?
A. Glacier County, home of the Blackfeet tribe.

Q. What invented adjective did Hillary Clinton use to describe Montana after her 1993 visit to the state?
A. "Hyper-rural," meaning extremely rural.

Q. What county seat, called the "lonesomest town in the world," is 175 miles from the nearest airport and 115 miles from the nearest rail depot?
A. Jordan of Garfield County, the most isolated county seat in the contiguous U.S.

Q. A driver on Highway 200 traveling the 300 miles between Lewistown and Sidney would encounter how many towns where gasoline is sold?
A. Three.

Q. What are the only two states that have a population density less than Montana, which has an average of 6.2 people per square mile?
A. Alaska and Wyoming. The national average is 75 people per square mile, and New York City has a density of 26,402 per square mile.

Q. What is the population density for both Petroleum and Garfield Counties?
A. 0.3 people per square mile.

Q. How many of Montana's 56 counties are considered to be "frontier counties" with an average population of six or fewer people per square mile?
A. 46.

Q. The 2000 Census showed that Treasure County lost six percent of its total population, ranking it ninth in the nation for highest percentage of population loss. How many people left Treasure County between 1990 and 2000?
A. 51.

Q. What county seat is the most urban with about 90,000 people?
A. Billings, seat of Yellowstone County, is the largest city in the state.

Q. What is the population density in Yellowstone County?
A. 48.3 people per square mile, the densest in the state.

Q. What percent of Montana land is considered by the Census Bureau to be metropolitan?
A. 5.5 percent, compared to 100 percent in Washington, D.C. and 0.3 percent in Alaska.

Q. How many towns have populations of 10,000 or greater?
A. Seven: Billings, Missoula, Great Falls, Butte, Bozeman, Helena, and Kalispell (in order).

Q. What percentage of Montana communities have populations of 3,000 or fewer?
A. 80 percent.

Q. How many different telephone area codes are there for Montana, the fourth largest state in the U.S.?
A. One: 406.

Q. The town of Ekalaka meaning "Swift One"
was named after a Native American girl born to the first white settler and his Oglala Sioux wife, who was grand-niece to what famous Sioux warrior?
A. Sitting Bull.

Q. The town of Dupuyer got its name from the French word for what part of a bison?
A. The back fat, considered a delicacy.

Q. The towns of Circle and Two Dot were both named after what?
A. Cattle brands.

Q. How many mine sites are there in the state?
A. 19,751, of which some 2,200 are still active.

Q. Montana has how many EPA Superfund sites?
A. 15, versus 116 in New Jersey, one in Washington, D.C., and none in North Dakota.

Q. How much metal was mined in Butte during the process of turning "the richest hill on earth" into the biggest toxic pit in the world?
A. 21 billion pounds of copper; 90 million pounds of molybdenum; 90 million ounces of silver, and 3 million ounces of gold.

Q. What percentage of Montana's mineral wealth is concentrated in Silver Bow County, where Butte is located?
A. 70 percent.

Q. In 1881 when the railroads were being built across Montana, how much track was laid in an average day?
A. One and a half miles per day.

Q. How many states had more land granted to a railroad than Montana's 17 million acres?
A. None. The Northern Pacific Railroad was given 40 square miles for every mile of track, which is about one-fifth of the state's land, equal in size to the state of West Virginia.

Q. In 1935, Montana had 5,194 miles of railroad line, more than any other Rocky Mountain state, but how many miles of line are there now?
A. Only about 3,300 miles.

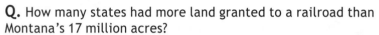

Q. What single product fills 74 percent of the rail cars leaving the state?
A. Coal, with farm products filling another ten percent and lumber accounting for five percent.

Q. Congress declared Yellowstone the nation's first national park in what year?
A. 1872.

Q. What two parks comprise the world's first International Peace Park?
A. Glacier National Park in Montana and Waterton Lakes in Alberta, Canada.

Q. What popular civic club with chapters across the U.S. and Canada promoted the idea of forming an International Peace Park?
A. Rotary Clubs across Alberta and Montana began circulating petitions in 1931 and the Peace Park was formed in 1932.

Q. How many glaciers are in Glacier National Park?
A. 48 small ones, the largest of which is Blackfoot Glacier at 420 acres.

Q. How many lakes are in Glacier National Park?
A. About 250.

Q. What percentage of the land in Glacier National Park is above the tree line?
A. 33 percent.

Q. What is the most prevalent type of rock found in Glacier National Park?
A. Limestone.

Q. What is the most prevalent type of rock found in Yellowstone National Park?
A. Volcanic.

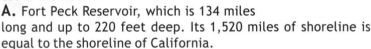

Q. What Montana reservoir is the fifth largest in the world?
A. Fort Peck Reservoir, which is 134 miles long and up to 220 feet deep. Its 1,520 miles of shoreline is equal to the shoreline of California.

Q. What is the largest natural freshwater lake west of the Great Lakes, with 124 miles of shoreline and 188 square miles of surface area?
A. Flathead Lake.

Q. How tall is the abandoned Anaconda Copper Mining Company smelter smokestack in Anaconda, the biggest freestanding masonry structure in the world?
A. 585 feet—the Washington Monument could fit inside it.

Q. How many pounds of sulphur dioxide did the Anaconda smokestack emit each day during its operation between 1883 and 1980?
A. 4.5 million pounds each day, along with 59,270 pounds of arsenic daily up until environmental controls were installed in 1976. The stack created the nation's largest EPA Superfund site.

Q. Why are juniper trees so prevalent throughout the Anaconda and Deer Lodge Valleys?
A. They are the only species of tree that can withstand the acid rain caused by sulphur dioxide.

Q. What town lies in both Montana and North Dakota?
A. Fairview. It claims to be the Sugar Beet Capital of both states.

Q. In 1904 when North Dakota was a prohibition state and Montana wasn't, in what town was there a bar built on the state line where you could buy a drink in Montana and consume it in North Dakota?
A. Sidney.

Q. What town was named for a popular six-year-old boy that everyone liked?
A. Sidney, named for Sidney Walters, the young son of early settlers.

Q. What town is almost in the exact geographical center of the state?
A. Lewistown is 12 miles east of the actual center of the state.

Q. Why is the easternmost town in the state called Westby?
A. Formerly the westernmost town in North Dakota, it was moved across the border when the railroad arrived; the suffix "-by" means "town" in Danish.

Q. A railroad man wanted to name a small town in the eastern part of the state after his daughters, Mary and Isabelle, resulting in what town?
A. Ismay, with a population of 26, making it the smallest incorporated town in the state.

Q. What town had the highest percentage of voter turnout in the entire state during the 2001 elections?
A. Ismay, where five of the nine registered voters unanimously returned Gene Nemitz to the mayor's office.

Q. How much does the mayor of Ismay earn for fulfilling the mayoral duties?
A. Four dollars a month.

Q. When officials at Great Northern Railroad in St. Paul needed to name stations along their new High Line, they did it by spinning a globe blindfolded and putting a finger on a spot, resulting in what towns?
A. Malta, after the Mediterranean island; Haarlem, Netherlands (now Harlem); Glasgow, Scotland; Dunkirk, France; and Saco, after a town in Maine.

Q. What is the only state that has more acres of land being farmed than Montana's 58.6 million acres?
A. Texas, with 129 million cultivated acres— after Montana come Kansas, Nebraska, and South Dakota.

Q. What percentage of Montana land is involved in farming or ranching?
A. 63 percent, ranking Montana second nationally after Texas.

Q. How many states harvest more wheat than the six million acres grown in Montana each year?
A. Only two: North Dakota and Kansas.

Q. What is the only state to produce more barley than Montana?
A. North Dakota.

Q. What county ranks first for highest agricultural income in the state?
A. Yellowstone County, with Billings as the county seat.

Q. Montana exports what percentage of its wheat to foreign countries?
A. 70 percent.

Q. How many ranchers live in Montana?
A. About 24,000, just under three percent of the population.

Q. What is their average age?
A. 60.

Q. Farming employs what percentage of Montana's work force?
A. 5.9 percent, compared to 1.9 percent nationwide.

Q. What is the only economic sector in which Montana's average wages are higher than the U.S. average wages?
A. Farming.

Q. Glacier County, encompassing the Blackfeet Indian Reservation, claims the world's highest per acre yield of what crop?
A. Flax.

Q. What county, in the heart of the wheat-rich area known as the Golden Triangle, produces the most winter wheat?
A. Chouteau.

Q. In 1901 at the height of sheep ranching in Montana, when there were 25 times as many sheep in the state as there were humans, how many sheep were there?
A. Six million, making Montana the top sheep producing state in the nation.

Q. How many sheep graze in the state now?
A. 360,000, ranking the state sixth in the nation.

Q. The Hutterites, a communal sect of German descent related to the Amish and Mennonites, maintain how many colonies across the state?
A. About 40, with about 4,000 total members and another 28,000 spread across Canada and the United States.

Q. How much of the state's pork is produced by the Hutterites?
A. 60 percent, along with 50 percent of the eggs and 17 percent of the milk.

Q. What town prompted Frank Burke to write, "You can never judge anything in these Western places by their names, for the people seem to have a peculiar habit of giving high-sounding names to the most insignificant places"?
A. Superior.

Q. Claude Carter decided to set up a saloon but on his way, when his wagon bogged down in mud and snow, he decided any place is a good place for a saloon, and built it on the spot— resulting in what town?

A. Ekalaka.

Q. How does Montana rank among states in terms of conservation easements protecting property from development?
A. Third, with 446,445 acres, behind California and New York. That's an area of about 700 square miles, or three-quarters the size of Rhode Island.

Q. Near what small town was the Unabomber, Ted Kaczynski, arrested after he had lived in a primitive and remote cabin nearby for more than 20 years?
A. Lincoln.

Q. What are the four largest industries in the state?
A. Agriculture (including crops and livestock), travel and tourism, timber, and mining.

Q. In what year did agriculture overtake mining as the state's number one business?
A. 1910, a year after the Enlarged Homestead Act gave settlers 320 acres.

Q. In terms of total economic impact, what are the three top agricultural products?
A. Wheat, barley, and hay.

Q. What are the top crops in terms of how much money they bring in per acre?
A. Potatoes, sugar beets, and dry beans.

Q. Fifty years ago Montana ranked in the top ten among states in per capita income, but where does it rank now?
A. 50th with an average per capita income of $26,000, compared to $46,852 in Connecticut, with the highest per capita income.

Q. What percent of residents live in poverty?
A. 14.6 percent, compared to 18.5 percent in Arkansas (the highest), and 6 percent in New Hampshire (the lowest).

Q. What percent of Montanans live in a home that they own?
A. 69 percent, compared to 77 percent in Minnesota (the most) and 50 percent in New York (the least).

Q. What is the average number of people per household in the state?
A. 2.45 people per home.

Q. Who is the largest employer in the state, employing 21 percent of the state's workforce?
A. The government, with 19,000 state employees, 34,000 local government employees, and 21,800 federal employees.

Q. What percentage of full-time jobs in the state capital, Helena, are related to running the state government?
A. 25 percent.

Q. What percent of the Montana population lives within a 250-mile radius of the capital city of Helena?
A. 70 percent.

Q. Malmstrom Air Force Base provides what portion of the economic base in Great Falls?
A. One-third.

Q. How many Minuteman missile silos are in the state?
A. 200, with each silo containing three warheads. Each missile has a range of 8,000 miles.

Q. How many states have more missiles than Montana?
A. None.

Q. What county reports the greatest number of UFO sightings per capita, according to the Computer UFO Network?
A. Wheatland, followed by Judith Basin and Cascade Counties. (Cascade County, home of Malmstrom AFB, has the greatest at 75, but CUFON is concerned with sightings per capita.)

Q. What is the average age of Montana residents?
A. 37 years old, compared to 27 for Utah (the youngest) and 39 for West Virginia (the oldest).

Q. What percentage of the state's population is more than 65 years old?
A. 13 percent, compared to Florida with 20 percent and Alaska with five percent.

Q. In what year did Montana lose one of its two seats in the U.S. House of Representatives when the census showed about 12,000 too few people to justify two seats?
A. 1990.

Q. Who did the voters elect to the U.S. House of Representatives in 2000, representing the second largest district in geographic area and the single most populous district in the nation?
A. Dennis Rehberg.

Q. The largest share of Montana's mining income comes from what?
A. Fossil fuels, especially coal.

Q. Coal lies underneath what percentage of land in Montana?
A. About 35 percent, part of what may be the largest coal basin on earth.

Q. If all Montana's coal reserves could be mined, and if the mines continued production at their current rate, when would the coal run out?
A. About 3,000 years from now.

Q. How many states produce more coal than Montana's 37 million tons annually?
A. Five: Wyoming, West Virginia, Kentucky, Pennsylvania, and Texas (in order).

Q. How many states produce more hydroelectric power?
A. Five: Washington, Oregon, New York, California, and Tennessee.

Q. Of the power generated in the state, how much is exported to other states?
A. About half.

Q. Residents of how many states consumed more energy per capita than Montana in the year 2000?
A. Only three: Alaska, Louisiana, and Wyoming. Hawaiians consume the least energy.

Q. Who had electricity first: Helena or New York City?
A. Helena, which was electrified in August of 1882, beat New York which got electricity in September of 1882.

Q. How many barrels of oil were produced in Montana in 2004?
A. 22 million barrels.

Q. How many barrels of oil were used worldwide in 2003?
A. More than 29 billion barrels. Montana contributed about 0.08 percent of the total.

Q. How does the state rank in production of gold?
A. Fifth, after Nevada, California, Alaska, and South Dakota.

Q. What tax was levied to mitigate the "plunder-and-run" tendencies of mining companies to abandon the people and the economy when the ore is gone?
A. The Coal Severance Tax, which brought in $66 million its first year in 1975 and today totals about $600 million.

Q. The town said to be named after the Pair-O-Dice Saloon is now called what?
A. Paradise.

Q. Hellgate, a narrow gap in the mountains east of Missoula that was named because many Indian battles in the area left it littered with bones, is how far away from Paradise?
A. It is 79 miles from Hellgate to Paradise.

Q. What town holds the state record for changing its name most often, having been known by such names as Stillwater, Eagle's Nest, and Sheep Dip?
A. Columbus.

Q. Where would you go to make authentic "rock" music, where each boulder on a mountain rings like a bell when hit with a hammer?
A. Ringing Rocks just northeast of Butte.

Q. How many acres are planted in mint each year in the state?
A. About 9,500.

Q. What percentage of Montana's mint is grown in the Flathead valley?
A. 90 percent.

Q. How much mint oil will a typical acre of mint plants yield?
A. 100 pounds, enough to flavor 1.25 million sticks of gum.

Q. How many acres of land are infested with the noxious weed knapweed?
A. Five million acres, spread across every single county.

Q. A typical knapweed plant can produce how many seeds each year?
A. Up to 18,000, and the seeds remain viable for seven to ten years.

Q. What product mined in Montana is used as a lubricant in drilling, for making kitty litter, in cosmetics, for body wraps and facial masks, in cement, and in hazardous waste treatment?
A. Bentonite, named after Fort Benton.

Q. What is the origin of bentonite, also known as fuller's earth?
A. Mineralized mud made of ancient volcanic ash.

Q. Bentonite was dumped into what nuclear reactor to detoxify the radiation after an accidental meltdown?
A. Chernobyl.

Q. Vermiculite, which was mined at Libby, is named after what?
A. Vermin, because it looks wormy (from the Latin *vermiculus* meaning full of worms).

Q. At the vermiculite mine in Libby, what companion mineral occurred with the vermiculite, contaminating a large area?
A. Asbestos.

Q. When a rare mineral called armalcolite was found in Garfield County, where was the only other place the mineral had ever been discovered?
A. Armalcolite, named for Apollo 11 astronauts Neil Armstrong, Aldrin, and Collins, was previously only found in Tranquility Base on the Moon. (It has since been found in other places.)

Q. Where would you find the only platinum mine in the U.S. along with the country's largest deposits of chrome?
A. South of Big Timber in the Stillwater complex.

Q. How many ferries still cross the Missouri River at remote locations where there is no bridge?
A. Three: Virgelle, Carter, and McClelland.

Q. What percentage of Montana's timberlands are privately owned?
A. 32 percent.

Q. What percentage of Montana land does the federal government own?
A. 29.5 percent.

Q. When four prospectors from New York were caught in a blizzard and agreed they had been crazy to have come to Montana, why did they name the spot after Utica, New York?
A. The New York Insane Asylum was there. Utica's current population is 25.

Q. The community of Glentana, population twelve, has one business (post office/store), two "exits" from rural route #248, and how many parking meters?
A. One, as a joke.

Q. The sign welcoming visitors to what town reads, "Home of 596 nice people and one old sorehead"?
A. Rudyard.

Q. What is the only part of the town of Canyon Ferry still visible above the waters of Canyon Ferry Lake, formed by Canyon Ferry Dam?
A. The cemetery on a hill that is now an island.

Q. While Billings has 450 miles of public roads within its city limits, how many does Rexford, population 132, have?
A. 1.38 miles, the least of any incorporated city in the state.

Q. Montana's cities contain how many miles of alleys?
A. 884, about the same as the driving distance from Alzada in the southeast corner of the state to Yaak in the northwest corner.

Q. Where is Montana's busiest stretch of road, with 47,970 vehicles passing by every day?
A. In Billings, on Main Street between 6th St. and Airport Road. (The busiest road in the U.S. is the East L.A. interchange where four freeways join. 443,000 cars go by every day.)

Q. The state's first highway, built in 1923, consisted of 26 miles of concrete connecting what two key mining towns?
A. Butte, where the ore was mined, and Anaconda, where the ore was smelted.

Q. When Lizzie Borden was on trial for murdering her parents with an axe, a prime suspect was the maid, Bridget Sullivan. After the trial in Massachusetts, what Montana town did Bridget flee to in 1897, seeking anonymity?
A. Anaconda.

Q. The most common collision on Montana highways occurs between two moving vehicles, but what is the second most common item to collide with?
A. Wildlife, with about 1,800 collisions per year.

Q. Recording a 40 percent growth from 1990 to 2000, what is the fastest growing county?
A. Ravalli in the Bitterroot Valley.

Q. In terms of birth rate, while Utah and California have the highest and West Virginia and Maine have the lowest, were does Montana rank?
A. Low, at number 43.

Q. What percent of residents of the state are parents?
A. 50 percent.

Q. What was the town of Clyde Park named after?
A. Clydesdale horses that were being raised there.

Q. Each day, how many flights leave Logan Airport in Billings, the busiest airport in the state?
A. About 30, compared to about 1,700 takeoffs and landings at Los Angeles International Airport daily (the second busiest in the nation).

Q. What man-made construction was featured on the cover of the very first issue of "Life" magazine in November 1936?
A. Fort Peck Dam.

Geography Crossword

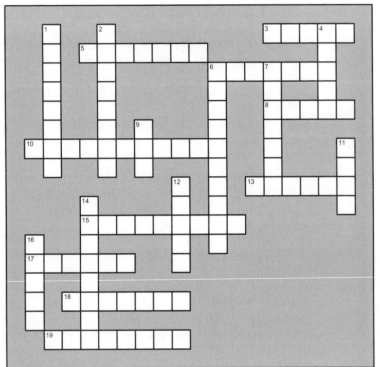

Created with the help of Wordsheets - www.Qualint.com

Across

3. How does the state rank in production of gold
5. The fastest growing county
6. Where do you find some of the oldest rocks on earth
8. What animal was there 25 times more of in 1901 than humans
10. What creek marks the first major gold strike in Montana
13. What is the capital of Montana
15. What type of rock is most often found in Glacier National Park
17. What town was named for a popular six-year old boy
18. What is Montana's second highest range
19. What is the largest freshwater lake west of the Great Lakes

Down

1. The nation's longest river
2. The town named after the Pair-O-Dice saloon
4. How many gas stations are there on Highway 200 between Lewistown and Sidney
6. Who is the largest employer in the state
7. What county has had the greatest number of UFO sightings
9. What is the world's shortest river listed by the Guiness Book of Records
11. What single product fills 74 percent of the rail cars leaving Montana
12. What Montana city had the largest population in 1917
14. Town with one parking meter
16. A railroad man wanted to name a small town after his daughters. What is the name that resulted.

Answers on page 152

SCIENCE AND
NATURE

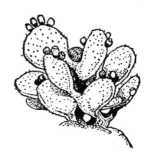

Q. How many states have a greater number of mammal species than the 109 kinds that live in Montana?
A. None.

Q. Where is the largest known concentration of free-roaming wildlife in the lower 48 states?
A. Yellowstone National Park.

Q. The average square mile of Montana land is estimated to contain 1.4 elk, 1.4 pronghorn antelope, 3.3 deer, and how many humans?
A. Six.

Q. Montana contains how many different species of flowering plants?
A. About 2,500, 14 of which grow *only* in Montana.

Q. How many species of birds live in the state?
A. 389, compared to 606 in Texas (the most) and 296 in Hawaii (the least).

Q. How many species of cactus are in the state?
A. Four. Texas has 92 species of cactus, more than any other state.

Q. What plant was Meriwether Lewis referring to when he called it "one of the beauties as well as the greatest pests of the plains"?
A. Prickly pear cactus.

Q. How long are the claws on Montana's state animal?
A. Adult grizzly bears have four-inch claws.

Q. How many states in the lower 48 have a greater number of grizzly bears than Montana?
A. None.

Q. How many grizzlies are estimated to live in the northern Rocky Mountain region between Yellowstone Park and Waterton Park in Alberta, Canada?
A. About 950, compared to an estimated 30,000 in Alaska.

Q. What percentage of the original range of the grizzly in the lower 48 states is no longer occupied by grizzlies?
A. 98 percent.

Q. How many buffalo are estimated to live in Montana?
A. None, because only bison live in the American West and buffalo live mainly in Africa and Asia.

Q. How many bison are estimated to have roamed the plains of the American West in 1864?
A. 30 to 60 million, enough to stop trains for hours as the herds crossed the tracks.

Q. In 1883 when an expedition from the Smithsonian Institution spent six months searching Montana for a bison specimen for an exhibit at the museum, how many bison did they find?
A. 50.

Q. How long did it take to reduce the bison herds from millions to a few dozen?
A. Seven years.

Q. In what year did the Montana Territory make it unlawful to kill game animals for hides alone, leaving the meat to rot?
A. 1877, 12 years before Montana became a state.

Q. When was the first federal legislation enacted to protect bison?
A. 1894.

Q. How many bison live on the nearly 19,000-acre National Bison Range near Moiese?
A. About 580 bison live on the nation's first wildlife refuge.

Q. What is the deepest lake in the state?
A. The Berkeley Pit in Butte, the largest open-pit copper mine in the world, now abandoned, is 900 feet deep and getting deeper.

Q. How many gallons of acid mine wastes and toxic groundwater are added to the Berkeley Pit every day?
A. Five million gallons.

Q. How many migrating snow geese died from drinking the water of the Berkeley Pit while migrating through in 1995?
A. 342— the water turned their snow-white bodies brownish-orange.

Q. There are around 250 miles of streets in Butte and how many miles of underground mining tunnels?
A. More than 2,500.

Q. What is the deepest *natural* lake in the state?
A. Tally Lake near Whitefish is 500 feet deep. Lake McDonald in Glacier National Park is about 470 feet deep, and Flathead Lake is 390 feet deep.

Q. Are there more cows or humans living in the state?
A. Cows, outnumbering humans almost three to one.

Q. Including all domestic food animals, what it the ratio of livestock to humans in Montana?
A. 12 to one.

Q. Approximately how much time does a cow spend eating each day?
A. Six and one half hours, consuming 25 pounds of hay and 10 gallons of water daily.

Q. What are the two most popular breeds of cattle in the state?
A. Black Angus and Hereford.

Q. What town bills itself as the "cow capital of the world"?
A. Miles City.

Q. What town proclaims itself to be a "world famous bull shipper"?
A. Drummond.

Q. Dead since 1910, where is Big Red, the last ox to pull freight over Bozeman pass?
A. His stuffed remains are displayed at the Powderhorn, a sporting goods store in Bozeman.

Q. The world's largest steer, which attained a height of 5 feet, 11 inches; a length of 10 feet, 4 inches; and a weight of 3,980 pounds, was born in what Montana town?
A. Baker, where the red roan shorthorn steer is now stuffed and on display at the O'Fallon County Museum.

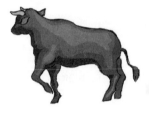

Q. At what junction would you find the state's largest fiberglass and Styrofoam cow, standing 15 feet high and 18 feet long?
A. Clearwater Junction.

Q. For many years, outside the Prairie Schooner Restaurant in what town were tourists entertained by two 12-foot-tall oxen statues that would "urinate" whenever someone in the restaurant turned the secret handle?
A. Three Forks.

Q. How can mountain goats be used to predict the weather?
A. If they're high on the mountain, the weather will be good, but when they move to low-lying areas, storm's a-comin'.

Q. The mountain goat is not a goat at all but instead is related to what animal?
A. Antelope.

Q. The pronghorn antelope is not a type of antelope but is related to what animal?
A. Goat.

Q. What animal is the fastest in North America and second fastest in the world?
A. Pronghorn antelope, outrun only by the cheetah.

Q. A pronghorn can cover what distance in a single running stride?
A. 20 feet.

Q. In Montana, "where the deer and the antelope play," how many pronghorn are estimated to live?
A. Around 200,000.

Q. In 1925 after a few decades of heavy hunting, how many pronghorn were living in the state?
A. About 3,000.

Q. What simple human invention used by farmers and ranchers devastated the pronghorn population?
A. The barbed wire fence, which pronghorn will not jump over.

Q. What was Lewis and Clark's first contact with the ponderosa pine, now the state tree?
A. While still in North Dakota they encountered its pinecones, which had drifted hundreds of miles downstream.

Q. Where would you find the largest known ponderosa pine in the state, at 194 feet tall and 78 inches wide?
A. Fish Creek Road, between Alberton and Superior.

Q. What conifer has bark resembling jigsaw puzzle pieces that pop off in forest fires to shed heat?
A. Ponderosa pine.

Q. What conifer found in western Montana sheds its needles every fall and grows new ones every spring?
A. Western larch, which can grow up to 200 feet tall and live 400 years.

Q. What has happened to the population base of western larch in the northern Rockies in the last half century?
A. It has decreased by 72 percent largely due to forest management practices that favor other species.

Q. How did the common Montana pine species Douglas fir get its name?
A. From Scottish botanist David Douglas who identified it in 1826.

Q. How long can a sagebrush plant live?
A. 200 years.

Q. A sudden warm wind in the winter that sweeps down from the mountains and melts the snow at a phenomenal rate has what name?
A. Chinook, a Native American word meaning "snow-eater."

Q. What town holds the national record for the greatest increase in temperature in 24 hours for a 103-degree rise on January 14, 1972?
A. Loma, which went from 54 below zero to 49 above zero the following day, the largest temperature swing ever in the nation.

Q. What town holds the national record for the greatest drop in temperature in twenty-four hours, for a 100-degree drop on January 23, 1916?
A. Browning, where the temperature went from 44 above to 56 below zero when an arctic cold front swept down from Canada.

Q. On January 11, 1980, when Great Falls set a new national weather record for quickest temperature increase in the shortest time, how long did it take to go from 32 below zero to 15 above?
A. Seven minutes.

Q. How many privately owned bison ranches are located in the state?
A. About 100.

Q. What media mogul, thought to be the largest private land-owner in the United States, owns large ranches in Montana where he raises about 4,000 bison?
A. Ted Turner, whose approximately 30,000 head across the western U.S. make him the largest bison producer in the country, owning about ten percent of the nation's herd.

Q. What fish was thought to be extinct until a man accidentally caught one in the Missouri River in 1962 near Fairview?
A. The paddlefish, which can weigh one hundred pounds.

Q. The paddlefish is found in only one other country in the world. Name it.
A. China.

Q. How many paddlefish licenses are granted in Montana each year?
A. About 2,000, including 550 for the Missouri River and 1,450 for the Yellowstone River.

Q. Paddlefish, who eat plankton, cannot be caught with a worm on a hook, so how are they caught?
A. By snagging, which is jerking a hook through the water until it snags the fish.

Q. Where is the 98-acre wildlife refuge specifically set aside for prairie dogs?
A. Greycliff Prairie Dog Town State Park, on I-90 near Big Timber.

Q. Of the 700 million acres across the Great Plains that were inhabited by prairie dogs in the 1880s, what percentage is still home to prairie dogs today?
A. Less than one percent.

Q. What nearly extinct animal— the rarest mammal in North America—relies on the prairie dog as a source of food and shelter?
A. The black-footed ferret. About 1,000 live in captivity and another 80 live in the wild.

Q. Where were endangered black-footed ferrets released when they were reintroduced into Montana in 1994?
A. The UL Bend National Wildlife Refuge south of Malta.

Q. When the Lewis and Clark expedition spent one entire day trying to capture a live prairie dog to be sent back to Washington, how did they finally make the catch?
A. By forming a bucket brigade and pouring water down its hole until it was flushed out—it survived the trip to Washington, D.C.

Q. What is the second largest wildlife refuge in the lower 48 states at 1.1 million acres?
A. Charles M. Russell National Wildlife Refuge wrapping around Fort Peck Lake. (Desert National Wildlife Range north of Las Vegas is the largest at 1.5 million acres.)

Q. How many wildlife refuges are there in the state?
A. 21.

Q. Alaska ranks first among states in the greatest number of acres set aside as national parks and historic areas. Where does Montana rank?
A. Eighth. (Delaware is 50th.)

Q. What percentage of the grizzlies that live in the northern Rocky Mountain region die of natural causes?
A. 10 percent, and the other 90 percent are killed, accidentally or intentionally, by humans.

Q. On average, how many humans are killed by grizzlies on the North America continent in a typical year?
A. One.

Q. On average, how many humans are killed by cows in North America in a single year?
A. 50. Another 45 will die by insect bites; 85 by lightning; and 12 by snakebite.

Q. What's the number one killer of Montanans?
A. Heart disease causes about 24 percent of all deaths in the state, with cancer a close runner-up. About 2,000 people die of each disease annually.

Q. What happened to the death rate due to diabetes in the state between 1950 and 2000?
A. It nearly tripled as the state's obesity rate steadily increased.

Q. What percent of traffic fatalities in the state are related to alcohol?
A. 49 percent, ranking the state sixth behind Rhode Island (55 percent), Hawaii, Nevada, North Dakota, and South Carolina. Utah is last with 15 percent.

Q. How many states have a higher highway fatality rate than Montana, with fatality rate defined as number of deaths per 100 million vehicle miles traveled?
A. Only one: Mississippi.

Q. What is the only other state whose average daily wind speed tops Montana's 12.7 mph?
A. Wyoming, with 12.9 mph.

Q. What city is the fourth windiest in the entire nation, coming in after Dodge City, Kansas; Amarillo, Texas; and Cheyenne, Wyoming?
A. Great Falls, where the average annual wind speed is 13 mph, tying with Casper, Wyoming.

Q. What city was the first in the nation to own a wind-powered utility?
A. Livingston, where four 25-kilowatt wind-powered turbines were installed in 1981.

Q. What happened to Livingston's wind turbines three weeks after installation?
A. One was destroyed by the wind and the other three were shut down to prevent overloading by the wind.

Q. How many megawatts of Montana's energy comes from wind power?
A. 0.1 megawatts, compared to 2,042.6 megawatts in California.

Q. What mineral, now a state gemstone, clogged the sluice boxes of the El Dorado Bar near Helena, making miners angry?
A. Sapphires, which were considered worthless at the time.

Q. How many states have produced more gem-quality sapphires than Montana?
A. None, and Yogo sapphires are some of the highest quality in the world.

Q. What color are Montana sapphires?
A. Sapphires are colorless but various impurities color them not only blue but also green, yellow, pink, and orange.

Q. What is red sapphire called?
A. A ruby.

Q. What is the only gemstone that is harder than sapphire?
A. Diamond.

Q. What semi-precious gems were the Ruby Mountains named after?
A. Garnets, which were thought at the time to be rubies.

Q. Moss agate, one of Montana's two official gemstones, is a type of what mineral that composes twelve percent of the earth's crust?
A. Quartz, in all its forms the single most abundant mineral on earth.

Q. Where can you find an intense concentration of quartz crystals free for the digging?
A. Crystal Park in the Pioneer Mountains.

Q. What is the only North American gem to be included in the Crown Jewels of England?
A. The Montana Yogo Sapphire.

Q. What blue flower used to grow so abundantly that fields full of their blooms could be mistaken for lakes?
A. Camas, whose edible root was a staple of the Native American diet.

Q. What happens to the seeds of the cow parsnip plant when eaten by a bear?
A. They are 70 percent more likely to sprout than seeds that have not been eaten by a bear.

Q. What plant, which is the Montana state flower, can live for more than a year without water and can be revived even after being boiled, dried, or pressed?
A. The bitterroot, whose tenacity is reflected in its Latin name *Lewisia rediviva* with "Lewisia" being for Meriwether Lewis who cataloged it, and "rediviva" meaning "one who lives again."

Q. Of the 122 animal species cataloged by Lewis and Clark on their 8,000-mile long journey, what percent are now either endangered, at-risk, or under federal protection?
A. 40 percent.

Q. What edible delicacy flourishes in years immediately following forest fires, spawning a cottage industry?
A. Morel mushrooms.

Q. Where in Montana have more golden eagles been sighted in a single day than anywhere else in the nation?
A. Rocky Mountain Front, which is along their migration route.

Q. Which weighs more on a typical ten-to-twelve pound bald eagle: the skeleton or the feathers?
A. The skeletal structure weighs half a pound but the seven thousand feathers weigh a pound.

Q. What community has the highest elevation in the state?
A. Cooke City, an unincorporated town on the Beartooth Highway near Yellowstone, lies at 7,651 feet above sea level. (West Yellowstone is the highest *incorporated* town, at 6,670 feet.)

Q. When year-round temperatures are considered, what town is the coldest in the state?
A. Cooke City.

Q. The state record for the greatest snowfall in a season, with 418.1 inches, goes to what town?
A. Cooke City, for the winter of 1977-78.

Q. If only winter temperatures are considered, what is the coldest town in the state with an average January temperature of 5.7 degrees?
A. Westby, in the extreme northeastern corner of the state.

Q. What conservation club was founded by wilderness advocate Bob Marshall and some of his friends?
A. The Wilderness Society.

Q. Bob Marshall, after whom Montana's Bob Marshall Wilderness is named, gave what reply when asked, "How much wilderness does America really need?"
A. "How many Brahms symphonies do we need?"

Q. What percent of Montana land is federally designated wilderness?
A. 3.7 percent, which is 3,442,416 acres. That's about the size of Connecticut.

Q. How many states have more designated wilderness acreage than Montana?
A. Five: Alaska, California, Arizona, Washington, and Idaho.

Q. What forester and conservationist won the prestigious Bob Marshall Award bestowed by the Wilderness Society for presenting scientific evidence that clear-cutting harms the environment?
A. Arnold Bolle, Dean of the School of Forestry at University of Montana.

Q. How many species of trees are commercially logged in the Libby area, the wettest part of the state, which receives up to 40 inches of rain per year?
A. Eight.

Q. The nine contiguous counties in the western half of the state account for what percentage of the state's income from timber?
A. 80 percent.

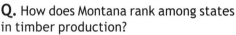

Q. How does Montana rank among states in timber production?
A. Fifth, behind Oregon, Washington, California, and Idaho.

Q. How many Douglas firs are cut each year in Lincoln County for use as Christmas trees?
A. 400,000.

Q. In Maine, 82 percent of the state is forested (the most in the nation) and in North Dakota only 1 percent (the least) but what percentage of Montana is forested?
A. 24 percent.

Q. What percentage of Montana's forested land is owned by the federal government?
A. 64 percent.

Q. How many smokejumpers are on duty with the Forest Service and the Bureau of Land Management each summer?
A. Around 400.

Q. Agriculture accounts for approximately what percentage of economic activity in the state?
A. 30 percent.

Q. What percentage of cash receipts from crops comes from wheat?
A. 68 percent.

Q. Which brings more into the state economy, wheat or cattle?
A. Cattle.

Q. What is the state grass, which grows from Alaska to Mexico and is useful for building soil and preventing erosion?
A. Bluebunch wheatgrass.

Q. What percent of the total mass of buffalo grass consists of roots?
A. 90 percent. The roots may go six feet straight down before branching out.

Q. How many place names, including towns, rivers, and mountains, have names relating somehow to grass?
A. 70, including Sweet Grass, Grassrange, Lodge Grass, and Grassy Mountain.

Q. What animal is the largest member of the deer family, weighing up to 1,200 pounds and eating more than 40 pounds of food daily?
A. Moose.

Q. Although in 1900 moose were thought to be extinct throughout Montana except in Yellowstone National Park, how many moose are estimated to live statewide now?
A. 8,000.

Q. How long can a moose keep its head under water?
A. Three minutes.

Q. At one time the fluvial Arctic grayling was found in all of the state's cold water streams, but what is its range today?
A. It is limited to the upper reaches of the Big Hole River.

Q. Considering year-round temperatures, what is the hottest town?
A. Thompson Falls in the northwest part of the state.

Q. Considering summer temperatures only, what is the hottest town?
A. Glendive, on the far eastern plains.

Q. How many states have a daily mean temperature lower than Montana's average year-round temperature of 44.6 degrees Fahrenheit?
A. Five: Vermont, Michigan, Minnesota, North Dakota, and Alaska.

Q. Where in Montana can the largest breeding population of trumpeter swans in the lower 48 states be found?
A. Red Rock Lakes National Wildlife Refuge.

Q. In 1932 there were 69 trumpeter swans breeding in the Yellowstone ecosystem, but how many are there today?
A. About 300, with another 2,000 stopping by during the migration.

Q. How many pounds of food will an average 20 to 30-pound trumpeter swan eat in a day?
A. 20 pounds of aquatic vegetation.

Q. The trumpeter swan at 40 pounds is the largest bird in the state, but what's the smallest?
A. The calliope hummingbird at 0.1 ounce.

Q. How many commercial hot springs are in the state?
A. 13.

Q. By chemical analysis, what hot spring is almost identical to the hot springs at Baden Baden, Germany?
A. White Sulphur Springs.

Q. What percentage of the total bison herd in Yellowstone was shot during the winter of 1996-97 when they strayed outside the park boundaries, for fear they would transfer brucellosis to cattle?
A. More than 33 percent, or more than 1,000. Another 1,800 died inside the park due to harsh winter conditions.

Q. How many instances are there on record of bison transferring brucellosis to cattle?
A. None.

Q. How many bison currently live in Yellowstone?
A. About 4,000.

Q. Which has more protein, the meat of a cow, or the meat of a bison?
A. Bison meat has 30 percent more protein than beef, 70 percent less fat, and 59 percent less cholesterol.

Q. Which sex of bison has horns?
A. Both.

Q. George Henry Cowan, a medial researcher at the Bitterroot laboratories, was the fourth of the five men there who died in the 1920s of what disease, which they were trying to cure?
A. Rocky Mountain spotted fever, carried by ticks.

Q. What man, whose name is now synonymous with frozen foods, once worked in the Bitterroot Valley as a field naturalist for the U.S. Biological Survey?
A. Clarence Birdseye in 1909 studied which animals are carriers of ticks and Rocky Mountain spotted fever.

Q. What doctor who spent his life researching livestock diseases died in Butte in 1914 and had a disease that's carried by chickens and eggs named after him?
A. Dr. Daniel Salmon, remembered for salmonella.

Q. Will a person freeze to death faster in dry air or humid air?
A. Humid air—it wicks heat away faster, as does perspiration and precipitation.

Q. How cold was it at Rogers Pass on January 20, 1954, when Montana set the record for the coldest temperature ever recorded in the continental U.S.?
A. The thermometer registered 70 degrees below zero, the lowest temperature it was capable of recording.

Q. At 70 below zero, how long will it take an unprotected face to freeze?
A. Less than a minute.

Q. Which state has the highest recorded temperature: Florida, Hawaii, or Montana?
A. Montana at 117 degrees Fahrenheit, compared to 109 for Florida and 100 for Hawaii.

Q. From 70 below zero to 117 above, Montana has the greatest temperature range of any state with 187 degrees, but what state comes in second?
A. North Dakota with a range of 181 degrees. Alaska is third with 180 degrees.

Q. In 1982 when the grizzly bear was chosen the state animal by 50,000 school children, what was the runner-up?
A. Elk.

Q. How many states have a larger population of elk than Montana?
A. None. There are an estimated 150,000 in the state.

Q. Elk antlers, one of the fastest growing animal tissues known to science, can grow how much per day?
A. One inch.

Q. How much does a typical large pair of elk antlers weigh?
A. 40 pounds.

Q. How does Montana rank among the states in honey production?
A. Fifth, turning out 13 million pounds annually worth $9 million.

Q. During its lifetime, the average worker honeybee makes how much honey?
A. One-twelfth of a teaspoon.

Q. What national monument on BLM land was created by presidential proclamation in 2001?
A. Upper Missouri River National Monument, where the river remains virtually the same as when Lewis & Clark traveled through the area.

Q. When a 2001 U.S. Fish and Wildlife survey found that Montana leads the nation with the largest percentage of birdwatchers, what state came in second place?
A. Vermont, where 43 percent of the population watches birds, came in second to Montana's 44 percent. (Hawaii came in last with 9 percent.)

Q. How many other states have the same state bird as Montana?
A. Five: Nebraska, North Dakota, Kansas, Oregon, and Wyoming all call the western meadowlark their state bird, a tie for top popularity with the cardinal.

Q. What caused some Montanans to be so dissatisfied with the western meadowlark as a state symbol that there was a major push in the 1980s to replace it with the black-billed magpie?
A. The meadowlark migrates and leaves the state every winter, but the magpie stays all year.

Q. Why was the magpie turned down as a possible replacement state bird?
A. Because it is an omnivorous scavenger and often feeds on carcasses.

Q. How many times per minute can a meadowlark repeat its call?
A. 200.

Q. Of the five species of tern found statewide, which is found the least?
A. The least tern, an endangered species in Montana found only near Fort Peck Dam.

Q. How many grasshoppers can a whooping crane eat in a single hour?
A. 800.

Q. How long does it take a typical flock of buzzards to pick clean a freshly dead antelope?
A. 20 minutes.

Q. How much does it cost to put out a forest fire per acre on average?
A. $1,164.

Q. How many acres burned in Montana during the summer of 2000, one of the hottest fire seasons in the history of the state?
A. 884,666—an area larger than the state of Rhode Island.

Q. What percentage of those acres burned because of human-caused fires?
A. About 20 percent.

Q. In general, about what percentage of Montana's forest fires are started accidentally by humans?
A. A little less than 50 percent, the rest being caused by lightning.

Q. What percentage of the state's total land area burned in 2000?
A. Less than one percent.

Q. At what temperature will the resin on the lodgepole pine cone melt, allowing the seeds to be released?
A. Between 113 and 140 degrees, achievable only in a fire.

Q. What percentage of the trees in Yellowstone are lodgepole pine?
A. 80 percent.

Q. How many lodgepole pine seeds does it take to weigh a pound?
A. 94,000.

Q. How many years after a forest fire will the greatest number of plant and animal species be found in a forest?
A. 25 years.

Q. At what age does a ponderosa pine begin bearing pinecones?
A. Usually between the age of 10 and 20, after which they can drop about 350,000 seeds per acre per year.

Q. When mountain pine beetles infest a weakened pine tree, how long will it generally take before the tree is dead?
A. One year.

Q. What's the latest high-tech weapon used to combat the mountain pine beetle?
A. Small packets containing a pheromone called "verbenone" which send out a chemical signal repelling beetles.

Q. What is the largest animal in Montana and the U.S.?
A. The bison, weighing up to 2,000 pounds.

Q. What wild animal species in Yellowstone National Park injures more humans than any other?
A. Bison, injuring an average of five tourists per year.

Q. The front teeth of a beaver can grow how much in a single month?
A. One inch.

Q. The beaver is the largest rodent in Montana, weighing up to 90 pounds, but what is the second largest rodent?
A. Porcupine, weighing up to 45 pounds.

Q. An average porcupine has how many quills?
A. 30,000.

Q. How much was the bounty placed on wolves in 1883?
A. One dollar.

Q. What cottage industry was spurred by the wolf bounty?
A. Breeding and raising wolf pups for fun and profitable bounty money.

Q. How many wolves were killed in Montana between 1883 and 1915?
A. 80,730.

Q. How many wolves live in the state now?
A. About 180.

Q. How many wolves live in Yellowstone?
A. About 130.

Q. In what year were wolves reintroduced to Yellowstone National Park?
A. 1995.

Q. How many states besides Montana maintain populations of wolves?
A. Seven: Idaho, Wyoming, Washington, Michigan, Wisconsin, Minnesota, and Alaska.

Q. How many instances are on record of a wolf killing a human?
A. None.

Q. On average, how many people are killed by dogs in a single year in North America?
A. 22.

Q. What is the best way to tell the difference between a grizzly bear and a black bear?
A. Through binoculars, look to see if the bear has a hump between its shoulder blades, a concave nose and dish-shaped face, and smallish ears, indicating it's a griz.

Q. What is the *worst* way to tell the difference between a grizzly and a black bear?
A. Climb a tree, and if it climbs up after you, it's a black bear, and if it pushes the tree down, it's a grizzly.

Q. On average, how many of the two million visitors to Glacier National Park will be mauled by bears in a typical year?
A. Two.

Q. How often does a female grizzly mate?
A. Generally every third year.

Q. What percentage of Montana is home to the mule deer?
A. 90 percent.

Q. Why is it not possible to tell the age of a deer by the size of its antlers?
A. Antler size depends on nutrition.

Q. What is the average annual precipitation across the state of Montana?
A. 15 inches.

Q. What county holds both the record for heaviest average annual precipitation and for lightest average annual precipitation?
A. Sanders, where Bull River Valley averages 40 inches of rain while Lonepine gets only 10.

Q. What town holds the record for least precipitation in a single year?
A. Belfry, south of Billings, where only 2.97 inches fell in 1960.

Q. What city holds the record for the most precipitation in a single year?
A. Summit, on the southern border of Glacier Park, with 55.51 inches in 1953.

Q. What city holds the record for greatest snowfall in 24 hours; greatest snowfall in four days; greatest snowfall in five days; and the greatest snowfall in one month?
A. Summit, when 131 inches of snow fell in January of 1972.

Q. What are the only two cities of significant size that have never seen snowfall in July or August?
A. Havre and Miles City.

Q. How many people were killed by avalanches in Montana between 1980 and 2004?
A. 56, ranking the state fourth behind Colorado (139), Alaska (87) and Utah (59).

Q. What percent of avalanche victims in the U.S. are men?
A. 90 percent.

Q. What percentage of Montana's stream flow originates from melting snow?
A. 70 percent.

Q. Of all the water used in Montana, what percentage is used for irrigation?
A. 96 percent, compared to 1.8 percent used for domestic purposes.

Q. What Montana river is the only major undammed river in the lower 48 states?
A. The Yellowstone.

Q. What river carries the greatest amount of water in the state?
A. The Clark Fork, followed by the Kootenai, the Yellowstone, and the Missouri.

Q. What river is said to be "a mile wide, an inch deep, and runs uphill"?
A. The Powder, which contributes about five percent of the water gathered by the Yellowstone River, but accounts for 50 percent of the silt; hence the name.

Q. How was the Tongue River named?
A. It was named by Native Americans who noted that the river was "as crooked as the tongue of a white man."

Q. What unusual adaptation aids the survival of the axolotl, a type of salamander found in Madison County?
A. It retains its gills as long as water is available, but loses the gills and breathes air when water dries up.

Q. How many species of snakes live in Montana?
A. 10, only one of which is poisonous — the prairie rattlesnake.

Q. How may states have a larger number of Rocky Mountain bighorn sheep?
A. None.

Q. In 1960 Norman "Jeff" Holter of Helena invented what currently used medical device for which he never accepted any money?
A. The Holter Heart Monitor, used to record heart function during a variety of activities.

Q. What University of Montana graduate won the 1934 Nobel Prize for chemistry for the discovery of deuterium and then worked on the Manhattan Project, although he urged U.S. leaders not to drop the bomb on Japan?
A. Harold Urey.

Q. Helena inventors Bill Crane and Jerry Spencer created what product that was displayed at the solar power exhibit at the Smithsonian's National Design Museum in New York City in 1999?
A. Solar panels to power portable computers.

Q. What paleontologist is credited with uncovering more dinosaur fossils than anyone else in history?
A. Jack Horner, who works from his base at the Museum of the Rockies in Bozeman.

Q. What early explorer said of the Petrified Forest in Yellowstone that there were "peetrified birds sittin' on peetrified trees singin' peetrified songs in the peetrified air"?
A. Jim Bridger.

Q. What caused the population of Cut Bank to swell from 845 in 1939 to 4,539 in 1960?
A. The discovery of oil and gas. The current population is about 3,500.

Q. What national forest was the first in Montana and one of the first in the nation?
A. Bitterroot, formed in 1887.

Q. How many tornadoes occurred in Montana between 1950 and 2001?
A. 325, compared to 6,596 in Texas and one in Alaska.

Q. Is the climate in Montana milder east of the Continental Divide or west of it?
A. The area west of the divide has warmer winters and cooler summers.

Q. It is sunny in Montana what percentage of the time?
A. 51 percent, compared to 81 percent in Arizona and 23 percent in Alaska.

Q. How many times has Flathead Lake frozen over in the last 50 years?
A. Seven.

Q. Frank Cimrhakl of Roy began serving as a volunteer weather observer, taking daily weather measurements, in what year?
A. 1938, longer than anyone else in the nation.

Q. How many years did an abandoned sheepdog nicknamed "The Auditor" live in Butte's toxic Berkeley Pit despite all efforts to remove and adopt him?
A. 17 years, from 1986 till his death in 2003.

Q. At what museum would you find a jar of (dead) grasshoppers on display?
A. The jar, containing 1,850 grasshoppers that were removed from a single bundle of rye in the bad locust year of 1938, is on display at the O'Fallon Historical Museum in Baker.

SCIENCE & NATURE WORD SCRAMBLE

1. ETERPUMTR ANSSW   _ _ _ _ _ _ _ _ _   _ _ _ _ _

2. ATLYL EKAL   _ _ _ _ _   _ _ _ _

3. LSSNRDEEWI   _ _ _ _ _ _ _ _ _ _

4. CEAIRGL   _ _ _ _ _ _ _

5. RBYEEELK TPI   _ _ _ _ _ _ _ _   _ _ _

6. LAIURNBCSO   _ _ _ _ _ _ _ _ _ _

7. AMCSA   _ _ _ _ _

8. ETDLHAAF LAEK   _ _ _ _ _ _ _ _   _ _ _ _

9. PRIAIER ODG   _ _ _ _ _ _ _   _ _ _

10. SONIB   _ _ _ _ _

11. HIBRNOG EPSHE   _ _ _ _ _ _ _   _ _ _ _ _

12. GUALCTRERUI   _ _ _ _ _ _ _ _ _ _ _

13. GVONLINTIS   _ _ _ _ _ _ _ _ _ _

14. EIAMPG   _ _ _ _ _ _

15. REIYDSEB   _ _ _ _ _ _ _ _

16. PHSIPEAR   _ _ _ _ _ _ _ _

17. EENTOSYLWLO   _ _ _ _ _ _ _ _ _ _ _

18. NOSRIUDA   _ _ _ _ _ _ _ _

19. COHNOKI   _ _ _ _ _ _ _

20. SHDFPAILED   _ _ _ _ _ _ _ _ _ _

21. ELOATPEN   _ _ _ _ _ _ _ _

22. GRLYIZZ   _ _ _ _ _ _ _

Answers on page 152

HISTORY

Q. The word *Sioux* comes from a Chippewa word meaning "enemy," but what did the Sioux call themselves in their own language?
A. *Dakota*, meaning "allies."

Q. One Montana tribe called themselves the Absarokee, meaning "people of the big-beaked bird," but how was that translated by the American settlers?
A. "Crow."

Q. The Sioux word *Cheyenne* means what?
A. "People of alien speech."

Q. A tribe of Indians called themselves *selish*, now known as Salish, which is a word meaning what?
A. "People."

Q. A tipi using 10 to 20 bison hides could be set up in less than an hour, and it would last how long?
A. About six years. They were susceptible to high winds and fire.

Q. Why is it called a tipi?
A. It comes from the Dakota words *ti*, meaning "dwelling," and *pi*, meaning "used for."

Q. What did the feathers in an Indian war bonnet signify?
A. Each feather had to be earned through war feats or hunting success.

Q. What tribe is thought to be the only Plains tribe that never made war against the white man?
A. The Absarokees.

Q. Why did both cowboys and Indians customarily wear garments with fringes?
A. Because fringes wick rainwater away from the garment, helping it dry faster.

Q. What was the total cost of the entire Lewis and Clark expedition?
A. $38,000.

Q. Who was against the Lewis and Clark expedition, feeling it was a waste of money?
A. Albert Gallatin, Secretary of the Treasury (for whom a river and a county are named) initially refused to fund the journey.

Q. Which member of the Lewis and Clark party was mistaken for an elk by a near-sighted hunter in the party, and shot in the butt?
A. Lewis.

Q. How many members of the Lewis and Clark expedition died during the trip?
A. One, a man named Floyd, possibly from appendicitis, very early in the journey.

Q. Members of the Lewis and Clark expedition killed how many people?
A. One, or possibly two, in a confrontation with Blackfeet Indians over the attempted theft of guns and horses.

Q. What was the name of Lewis's pet Newfoundland dog, who accompanied them for the entire journey?
A. Seaman—Lewis named a creek in Montana after it, now know as Monture Creek.

Q. How much did Lewis earn for his efforts during the trip?
A. 40 dollars per month.

Q. How much did Clark earn?
A. 25 dollars per month.

Q. How much did the privates earn?
A. Five dollars per month.

Q. How much did Sacajawea (the female Indian interpreter) and York (Clark's personal slave) earn?
A. Nothing.

Q. What Shoshone woman has more mountains, lakes, and streams named after her than any other North American woman?
A. Sacajawea.

Q. How old was Sacajawea when she and her infant son joined the Lewis and Clark party?
A. 15 or 16.

Q. How many years after the Lewis and Clark expedition ended did it take William Clark to receive the promotion Lewis promised him, from lieutenant to captain?
A. 195 years. It was awarded by President Bill Clinton.

Q. What explorer was captured by Indians near the Missouri River headwaters, stripped, told to run for his life while they hunted him for sport, survived by hiding under a beaver lodge, then walked more than a week to reach help more than 200 miles away?
A. John Colter, who first came west with Lewis and Clark and later returned on his own.

Q. The town of Fallon was named for Benjamin O'Fallon, Indian agent, army officer, and nephew of what famous explorer?
A. William Clark.

Q. In 1854, Sir George Gore, a wealthy Irish bachelor, traveled across the Rockies with his entourage; how many animals did he kill during the 11 months he spent in the Yellowstone River Valley?
A. 2000 bison, 1,600 deer and elk, 100 bears, and thousands of birds of every kind.

Q. How much money was appropriated by Congress in 1856 in a failed experiment to outfit western packers in Montana and other states with camel caravans to transport goods?
A. $30,000—horses and mules stampeded at the sight of the strange animals.

Q. The first steamboat arrived at Fort Benton in 1860, four came in 1862, but how many made the trip in 1867 at the peak of steamer travel?
A. 39, the final one arrived in 1888.

Q. What killed the steamboat business?
A. Advent of the railroads.

Q. What percentage of the steamboats that left St. Louis bound for Fort Benton via the Missouri River never made it back down the river?
A. 20 percent. They caught on fire, got stuck on sandbars, were captured by Indians, had their boilers blow up, and were otherwise damaged or destroyed.

Q. With a town and a county now named for him, what president of the American Fur Company brought the first steamboat up the Missouri?
A. Pierre Chouteau—the town is spelled Choteau.

Q. During the twelve years it did business in the early 1800s, the Rocky Mountain Fur Company shipped $50,000 worth of beaver pelts to St. Louis, but had how many dollars' worth of goods, furs, and horses stolen?
A. $100,000.

Q. What caused an American Fur Trading Company steamboat to explode catastrophically near Wolf Point in 1861?
A. A deckhand tried to tap a keg of alcohol by candlelight and there were 25 kegs of gunpowder on board.

Q. What disease was carried to the Native Americans from an infected steamboat crew that docked near the future site of Fort Benton in 1837, devastating tribes across the state?
A. Smallpox.

Q. When a smallpox epidemic swept through the vulnerable Blackfeet tribe in 1837, how many were killed?
A. 6,000, which was two-thirds of the tribe.

Q. How many bison hides were shipped from Montana to St. Louis in 1873?
A. 1,508,000.

Q. How many bison hides were shipped from Montana to St. Louis one year later, in 1874, following wholesale slaughter of bison?
A. 158,000.

Q. What time was it for 115 years in Fort Benton after money ran out in 1884 as the courthouse was being built, so a fake clock made of plywood was installed in the clock tower?
A. 12:20—until schoolchildren raised the $750 for a real clock in 1999.

Q. A trail between Fort Benton and Canada got what name after a trader was asked how things were going on the trail and he replied, "They're sure whoopin' it up" referring to Indians trading for whisky?
A. The Whoop Up Trail.

Q. It was illegal to take alcohol onto Indian reservations, so smugglers would hide flasks in their boots, giving us what word for illegal alcohol?
A. Bootleg.

Q. How many military forts were built in Montana between 1807 and 1885?
A. 99, more than one per year.

Q. What was the final fort established in the state, now a veteran's hospital and National Guard training ground located outside Helena?
A. Fort Harrison, built in 1892.

Q. How long did it take John Mullan and his 250-man crew to build a road that reached 624 miles from Fort Benton to Walla Walla, Washington?
A. Three years, 1859-1862.

Q. How much did it cost to build the Mullan Road, the last link in the transportation route between the Atlantic and the Pacific?
A. $100,000.

Q. A century later, how much did it cost to create the interstate system in Montana?
A. $1.2 billion.

Q. After the completion of the Mullan Road, how long did it take the average party to travel its 624 miles?
A. 47 days.

Q. When six prospectors dipped their gold pans in Alder Creek in 1863, leading to one of history's richest placer gold discoveries, how much gold were they hoping to find?
A. Enough to pay for their tobacco.

Q. The $10 million worth of gold taken out of Alder Creek, which runs through Virginia City and Nevada City, would be worth how much in today's value?
A. $2.5 billion.

Q. The population of Confederate Gulch near Helena went from zero to 10,000 in six years after gold was found, but in the seventh year, what was the population?
A. 64—the gold ran out and it is now a ghost town.

Q. At what place did 20 miners pan 700 pounds of gold from a two-acre claim in a single day?
A. Confederate Gulch.

Q. What ghost town was completely emptied of its 3,000 residents in less than two days when the silver panic of 1893 sent prices plummeting?
A. Granite, near Philipsburg.

Q. What tribe was named for the Native American phrase meaning "stone boilers," referring to their habit of cooking meat by dropping heated stones into the stew?
A. Assiniboine.

Q. Built in 1879, what was the largest military fort west of the Mississippi, with 104 buildings housing 500 soldiers and their families?
A. Fort Assiniboine near Havre.

Q. General John Pershing of World War I fame was a first lieutenant while serving at what Montana fort?
A. Fort Assiniboine.

Q. Although in 1888 the town of Cypress boasted a store, a restaurant, two bordellos, and 32 saloons, why did it wither to nothing but a single saloon in 1889?
A. The commanding officer of nearby Fort Assiniboine declared it off-limits to the troops.

Q. What shorter route to the gold fields of Montana cut 400 miles from the trip but traversed ceded Indian lands, leading to resentments that led to the Battle of the Little Big Horn?
A. The Bozeman Trail. 90 percent of overland travel passed this way until hostile Indians closed it down.

Q. The largest number of Indians ever gathered together for a single battle fought which battle in Montana?
A. Battle of the Little Big Horn, known as Custer's Last Stand. Indian numbers were estimated from 10,000 to 15,000, including more than 2,500 warriors.

Q. How many of General Custer's unit of 215 men survived the Battle of the Little Big Horn on June 25, 1876?
A. One, a scout named Curly, plus a horse named Comanche. About 100 Indian warriors also died.

Q. How did George Armstrong Custer rank in his class when he graduated from West Point?
A. Dead last.

Q. What members of George Custer's family were killed along with him at the battle of the Little Big Horn?
A. His brothers Tom, George, and Boston, his brother-in-law James Calhoun, and his nephew Autie Reed.

Q. What was the temperature on January 23, 1870, when 200 cavalrymen opened fire on a Blackfeet village, killing 173 men, women, and children, and leaving 140 survivors to walk 90 miles for help?
A. It was 35 below zero during the Baker Massacre— the cavalry suffered one fatality.

Q. What running Indian battle in 1877, covering more than 1,000 miles through Oregon, Idaho, Wyoming and finally Montana, became the first Indian war to be reported on a daily basis by telegram, and was the last major Indian conflict in the U.S.?
A. The Flight of the Nez Perce, which resulted in the deaths of 171 warriors and 148 women and children.

Q. Upon surrender, only 40 miles short of freedom at the Canadian border, what Indian chief declared, "From where the sun now stands, I will fight no more forever"?
A. Chief Joseph of the Nez Perce.

Q. When townsfolk wanted to name one of the state's first towns Varina in honor of Jefferson Davis's wife, Union supporter Judge Bissell refused and named it what instead?
A. Virginia City.

Q. Henry Plummer's day job in the 1860s was to serve as the first sheriff of Montana Territory, but what was his night job?
A. He headed a band of highway robbers called "The Innocents" and was hanged for it in 1864, although some historians feel he was innocent.

Q. Henry Plummer and his gang were credited with killing how many people?
A. 102.

Q. Angry vigilantes hanged how many members of Henry Plummer's gang, without benefit of trial?
A. 28.

Q. What town founder was so mean that it's said when he died, townsfolk buried him six feet deeper than normal and piled rocks on his grave to prevent him from getting out?
A. Pike Landusky, founder of Landusky.

Q. In 1894 what famous outlaw shot and killed Pike Landusky in front of Jew Jake's saloon?
A. Kid Curry—it was his first crime.

Q. Near Malta on July 3, 1901, what three outlaws held up the Great Northern Number 3 passenger train?
A. Kid Curry, Butch Cassidy, and the Sundance Kid.

Q. When the delegates to the first territorial legislative assembly met for 60 days in 1864 in Bannack to pass laws governing the new territory, how many pages did their new laws fill?
A. 700.

Q. Where is the original constitution of Montana?
A. No one knows, as it was lost, supposedly on its way to St. Louis to be printed.

Q. How many times was the state constitution amended between 1889 and 1970?
A. 41—in 1972 a new constitution was adopted.

Q. A law passed by the territorial legislature in 1872 made it illegal for people of what nationality to own mining property?
A. Chinese—the law was repealed in 1874.

Q. How long did Irish miner Thomas Cruse dig before he uncovered the mother lode at the Drumlummon mine near Marysville, from which gold worth some $50 million was extracted?
A. Six years.

Q. Thomas Cruse donated $200,000, or a third of the cost, to build Helena's cathedral and also carried the bonds that financed the building of what Montana landmark?
A. The Capitol building.

Q. Whose funeral mass was the first held in the St. Helena Cathedral?
A. Thomas Cruse's.

Q. Why is it ironic that the wrought iron fence that once surrounded Thomas Cruse's mansion now decorates the public library?
A. Thomas Cruse never learned to read.

Q. After Nate Vestal made a fortune from the Penobscot gold mine near Helena, one of the richest in the world, he lost all his money in the stock market and then took what job?
A. Laborer in the mine he had once owned.

Q. After three of the four prospectors who first discovered gold in Helena spent three years mining, they cashed in their nuggets back east and received how much money?
A. $40,000 each, the fourth having sold his claims.

Q. Excavation for what building on Last Chance Gulch in Helena resulted in enough placer gold to pay for its construction?
A. The Placer Hotel.

Q. When a fire broke out in the Helena Brewery in 1870, how did the owners save the building from complete destruction?
A. By taking all the full kegs of beer to the roof and emptying them out.

Q. The first schoolhouse in Flatwillow, a log cabin built in 1900, was a school by day and what by night?
A. A saloon.

Q. In Terry in the late 1890s, why was it impossible to hold school during sheep-shearing season?
A. Because until 1897 the schoolhouse was also the wool house.

Q. Charles Bair, who owned some 300,000 sheep (thought to be the largest flock in the nation) filled how many railroad cars with his wool in 1905?
A. 44, about 1.5 million pounds of wool, worth about $1,635,000.

Q. Why did Walter Winnett, after whom the town of Winnett was named, build the Log Cabin Saloon on his property?
A. To keep his ranch hands from sneaking his horses out to ride over to Grass Range for a drink.

Q. Disgruntled miners gave what names to three temporary mining camps near Radersburg?
A. Hog-Em, Cheat-Em, and Rob-Em.

Q. Where was the silver ore that was mined in Clancy taken to be smelted in the late 1800s?
A. By wagon it went to Fort Benton, by steamer to St. Louis, and by freighter to Swansea, Wales—and still netted a profit.

Q. What copper baron resigned his U.S. Senate seat in 1899 after being accused of buying votes and threatened with investigation?
A. William A. Clark of Butte, who was re-elected without scandal in 1893.

Q. In the 1880s when copper king William Clark, the richest person on earth, was earning $17 million a month from his mine holdings, how much were the workers in his mines earning?
A. $3.50 per day.

Q. How many years did wages remain a maximum of $3.50 per day for underground miners in Butte?
A. Around 40 years, until they got a raise in 1917 to $5.25 per day.

Q. How many underground miners were working in Butte in 1917?
A. Around 18,000 working in 138 different mines.

Q. After attending a dinner in honor of copper king Senator William A. Clark, what was Mark Twain's opinion of the richest man on earth?
A. Twain wrote, "He is as rotten a human being as can be found anywhere on earth."

Q. What technological advance led to a great need for copper in the 1870s?
A. The development of electricity, which required copper wiring to carry current.

Q. What technological advances led to the collapse of the copper market a century later?
A. The invention of fiber optic cable for communication and PVC pipe for plumbing.

Q. What percentage of the nation's copper was provided by the Butte mines in the 1880s?
A. 30 percent of the nation's copper, and 15 percent of the world's copper.

Q. Pushed by the miners' union in Butte, the eight-hour day for miners became law in Montana in what year?
A. 1901, four years after being proposed to the legislature.

Q. What was William A. Clark referring to when he credited it for giving the women of Butte clear complexions?
A. Arsenic in the smoky air.

Q. What served as an air filter in the early days of the lead smelter in East Helena?
A. Fumes passed through 3,000 woolen bags.

Q. When the uranium mines around Boulder were depleted and the mines were closed, what cottage industry grew up?
A. Radon health mines, where people hope to cure illnesses by exposing themselves to low-level radiation in the mine tunnels.

Q. In 1897 Lieutenant James Moss at Fort Missoula had his troops try out what method of transportation for troop movements?
A. The bicycle.

Q. What sporting goods company, still in business today, provided Lieutenant Moss with bicycles and used his photos, notes, and reports in their advertisements?
A. Spaulding.

Q. How long after Montana was declared a territory in 1864 was the Montana Historical Society incorporated?
A. About seven months.

Q. When a circus elephant sat down in a ditch, blocking the water flow used for power generation, what town went without power briefly in 1902?
A. Big Timber.

Q. At what town in 1921 did lightning strike a group of circus elephants, killing one who was given a full funeral and buried on the spot?
A. Dillon, where the grave can still be seen at the fairgrounds.

Q. While the 2000 Census showed slightly more than 900,000 people living in the state, how many lived in the Montana Territory at the time of the first census in 1870?
A. 20,595.

Q. What Irish rabble-rouser was convicted of treason, sentenced to life imprisonment in the penal colonies of Tasmania, escaped, fled to America, became a lawyer, editor, and major general, and served as acting governor of Montana Territory?
A. Thomas Francis Meagher, for whom a county is named.

Q. How do you pronounce Meagher?
A. "Mah-HARR" if you're Irish; "mar" if you're a Montanan; and "meager" if you're a tourist.

Q. Under what suspicious circumstances did Thomas Meagher die?
A. He fell or was pushed off a steamer at dock and his body was never found.

Q. How many governors of Montana came and went before a governor was elected who was actually born in the state?
A. Ten. The 11th, Roy E. Ayers (1937-41) was born in Fergus County.

Q. Before Montana Territory was formed in 1864, parts of it had been in how many other territories?
A. Seven: Louisiana, Missouri, Oregon, Washington, Nebraska, Dakota, and Idaho.

Q. What president issued the proclamation declaring Montana a state?
A. Benjamin Harrison.

Q. Where is the bell that is rung once per year, at precisely 10:40 a.m. on November 8?
A. At the state capitol—the Montana Statehood Centennial Bell commemorates the moment in 1889 when President Harrison signed the proclamation making Montana the 41st state.

Q. What is the meaning of the state motto *oro y plata*?
A. "Gold and Silver."

Q. What three tools appear on the state seal?
A. A pick, a plow, and a shovel.

Q. What three tools is a camper required to have when camping during fire season?
A. Shovel, axe, and bucket.

Q. When the North American Vexillogical Association studied the state flags of the nation in 2001, where did it rank Montana's flag?
A. In the bottom ten because it merely portrays the state seal.

Q. How long was Bannack the capital of Montana Territory before the capital was transferred to Virginia City?
A. About eight months, from May 26, 1864, to February 6, 1865.

Q. Virginia City was the territorial capital for how long before it moved to Helena?
A. 10 years.

Q. From 1892 to 1894 when Anaconda was fighting Helena for the right to become the state capital, how much money was spent on the campaign?
A. More than a million dollars, with Helena winning by a two percent margin.

Q. What's the annual salary of Montana's governor as of 2005?
A. $96,500 compared to $65,000 for Nebraska's governor and $179,000 for New York.

Q. What covers the dome of the Capitol Building?
A. Copper from the Anaconda Copper Company.

Q. The small town of Columbus enjoyed a streak of prosperity when stone from the local quarry was chosen to build what landmark?
A. The Capitol Building in Helena.

Q. How much did it cost to build the Capitol Building in Helena during 1899-1902?
A. $485,000.

Q. How much did it cost to restore and modernize the Capitol Building during 1999-2001?
A. $26 million.

Q. In the Butte mines, why were unstable slabs of rock that were prone to collapse without warning known as "duggans"?
A. Duggans was the most popular funeral parlor in Butte.

Q. When the carbide lamp of a foreman accidentally started a fire in the Speculator Mine in Butte on June 8, 1917, how many miners died?
A. About 168, making it the worst disaster in metal-mining history.

Q. How many miners died at the Smith Mine near Red Lodge when an explosion ripped through it on February 27, 1943, making it Montana's worst coal mine disaster?
A. 74. Most of the bodies were removed at night to avoid spectators. The mine was never re-opened.

Q. What happened in 1879 in Philipsburg when mine owners refused to pay the miners while requiring them to work anyway?
A. The miners seized control of the mine and worked until they had dug out enough ore to pay themselves.

Q. When the Montana Stock Growers Association was formed in 1884, what charter member later became president of the United States?
A. Theodore Roosevelt.

Q. When did Montana reach the peak of the open range boom, with 700,000 cattle and a million sheep?
A. 1886.

Q. What devastating winter was described by one cowboy as "hell without the heat"?
A. 1886-87.

Q. How many of the two hundred cattle operations went belly-up after the brutal winter of 1886-87 during which more than 350,000 cattle and innumerable sheep died?
A. 80, after 60 percent of the cattle in the state starved.

Q. How much did the average cowboy earn during the heyday of cattle operations on the open range, 1860-1885?
A. $30 per month.

Q. How much did cowboys earn in 1999?
A. An average of $10,151 per year, one of the lowest paid jobs in Montana.

Q. What ended the cattle drives from Texas to Montana?
A. The advent of the railroad.

Q. What mining town, founded by Marcus Daly, was originally known as Copperopolis?
A. Anaconda. Another Montana town already claimed the name Copperopolis.

Q. In Hamilton in the late 1800s, Anaconda Mining Company founder Marcus Daly built Riverside, the largest house in Montana, which had how many bedrooms?
A. 25, along with 15 bathrooms.

Q. What had velvet walls, brass railings, carpeted floors, modern plumbing and a hay rack?
A. The horse stall for Marcus Daly's prize racehorse, Tammany.

Q. When the Northern Pacific refused to stop their trains in town, locals piled logs on the tracks and, while the obstructions were being removed, boarded the trains to talk immigrants into disembarking and living in what town?
A. Thompson Falls.

Q. When John Ringling (of circus fame) built a railroad that extended only 21 miles from the town of Ringling, what was his defense when teased about its short length?
A. "It may not be as long as the others, but it's every bit as wide." The Ringling Brothers owned more than 100,000 acres in the area and once thought about moving their circus headquarters to Ringling.

Q. When USGS director John Wesley Powell reported to Congress in 1878, how many acres did he suggest were needed for a single homesteading family to make ends meet in eastern Montana?
A. 2,560.

Q. How many acres did Congress allow each family in the Free Homestead Act, signed by President Lincoln in 1862?
A. 160.

Q. How many acres did Congress allow each family in the Enlarged Homestead Act in 1909 when it became apparent that 160 acres was not enough?
A. 320, or half a square mile.

Q. How many acres is the average Montana farm today?
A. 2,714, slightly larger than John Wesley Powell's recommendation.

Q. Where was the very first homestead entry claimed in Montana?
A. In Helena, near the site of the Cooney Convalescent Home, filed in 1868 by David Carpenter.

Q. Were women allowed to file homestead claims?
A. Yes, if they were unmarried.

Q. How many settlers arrived on Montana's northern plains after the Enlarged Homestead Act in 1909 granted 320 acres to any settler able to live there five years?
A. 85,000.

Q. How many settlers left Montana following the drought of 1919?
A. 65,000.

Q. Of the 270 million acres that were claimed nationwide under the Homestead Act, Montanans claimed the most with 32 million acres. What state was second?
A. Nebraska with 22 million acres.

Q. What percent of western settlers who filed claims under the Homestead Act were successful in getting title to the land?
A. Only between one-third and one-half.

Q. When was the Homestead Act repealed?
A. 1976, except in Alaska where it was repealed in 1986.

Q. In 1909 there were 258,000 cultivated acres in the state; how many cultivated acres were there just 10 years later?
A. 3,417,000.

Q. How many loaves of bread can be made from an average bushel of wheat?
A. About 73.

Q. In the unusually wet year of 1916, some prairie farmers were able to raise 80 bushels of wheat per acre, but how many bushels did they average during the drought year of 1919?
A. Only 2.4 bushels per acres—modern farms average about 32 bushels.

Q. Compared to 1920 when there were 57,700 individual farms in the state, how many are there today?
A. There were 24,279 individual farms in the 1997 Census: 18,751 owned by individuals or families, and 123 corporate-owned.

Q. During the height of homesteading days, there were more than 200,000 Montanans involved in agricultural activities, compared to how many today?
A. About 98,099 people are employed by farming and ranching, representing 19.6 percent of Montana's total employment.

Q. What historic site in Deer Lodge re-creates the headquarters of one of the largest ranches in the country in the 1880s, a spread that covered more than 10 million acres, the size of Connecticut, Massachusetts, and Rhode Island combined?
A. The Grant-Kohrs Ranch.

Q. Where was the final target of Carry Nation who, in her anti-alcohol crusade, attacked bars with her hatchet?
A. Butte in 1910, where Nation was so badly beaten by barkeep and madam May Maloy that she retired from her temperance tantrums.

Q. When parking meters were installed, cowboys insisted on putting their money in them and tying their horses to them, causing controversy in what town?
A. Havre.

Q. How many people died in the state's worst fire season in 1910, when three million acres burned across Montana and Idaho?
A. 85, including many members of the fire crews who were never identified because they had been so hastily rounded up.

Q. On September 30, 1911, at Mullan Pass near Helena, how old was Cromwell Dixon when he became the first pilot to fly over the Continental Divide, thus winning a $10,000 prize?
A. 19.

Q. How long after that feat did Dixon die when his biplane crashed in a sudden burst of wind near Spokane?
A. Two days.

Q. What aviator was a barnstormer in Billings before he became famous?
A. Charles Lindbergh.

Q. David Williams, at age 21 the youngest man ever elected to the Montana state legislature, was the father of what famous 1940s leading lady?
A. Myrna Loy. He died in the flu epidemic of 1918.

Q. Ella Knowles, the first woman to pass the Montana bar exam, practice law, and plead a case before the U.S. Circuit Court, also ran for what political office?
A. State attorney general in 1892. She later married the man who defeated her.

Q. What year were Indians declared to be citizens of the United States?
A. 1924, with the Indian Citizenship Act.

Q. Women were given the right to vote nationwide in 1920, but when did women get the vote in Montana?
A. 1914.

Q. What champion of women's rights was the first woman to be elected to the U.S. Congress in 1916?
A. Jeannette Rankin of Missoula.

Q. What was Jeannette Rankin's first action as a representative?
A. She introduced a bill that would have allowed women citizenship independent of their husbands.

Q. How long after electing the first woman to Congress did Montana elect their first woman governor?
A. More than 80 years, when Judy Martz was elected in 2000.

Q. What county had Montana's first woman sheriff, Ruth Garfield, who served from 1920 to 1922?
A. Golden Valley, where she was appointed after her husband was killed in the line of duty.

Q. What was unusual about Mayor Gregory of Missoula, who installed the first street lamps and parking meters in the town in the late 1940s?
A. Mayor Juliet Gregory was the first (and only) female mayor of Missoula.

Q. In 1935 Bob Fletcher was able to convince the Highway Department to become the first state to do what?
A. Mount historical markers along the highways.

Q. How many historical markers are located around the state?
A. 173.

Q. Montana's (non-vanity) license plates start with a number between one and 56, with the numbers being each county's population rank in 1930. What are the first eight counties by license plate number?

A. 1. Silver Bow (Butte), 2. Cascade (GreatFalls),   3. Yellowstone (Billings), 4. Missoula, 5. Lewis and Clark (Helena), 6. Gallatin (Bozeman), 7. Flathead (Kalispell), and 8. Fergus (Lewistown).

Q. If the 2000 census were used to re-order the numbering of license plates, what would be the top eight counties, in order?
A. 1. Yellowstone, 2. Missoula, 3. Cascade, 4. Flathead, 5. Gallatin, 6. Lewis and Clark, 7. Ravalli, and 8. Silver Bow.

Q. How accurate was the original license plate numbering system?
A. Only counties one through four were accurate. The other 52 counties were numbered in a jumble, probably depending on who paid off whom.

Q. What percentage of the approximately 7,500 Native Americans living on the Crow Reservation speak Crow as their first language?
A. 85 percent.

Q. What chief represented the Indian Nation as head of state at the ceremony in Washington, D.C., to dedicate the Tomb of the Unknown Soldier?
A. Chief Plenty Coups of the Crow Tribe.

Q. What Montanan came closer than any other Montanan to securing the presidential nomination and later turned down the vice presidential nomination?
A. Senator Thomas Walsh in 1924.

Q. Longtime Montana Senator Thomas Walsh led the investigation that uncovered illegal and irregular oil leases that led to what national scandal in 1924?
A. Teapot Dome.

Q. What senator died on his honeymoon on a train on the way to Washington, D.C., to accept appointment as U.S. Attorney General?
A. Thomas Walsh, in 1933.

Q. Elected U.S. senator in 1934 to fill the vacancy formed by Thomas Walsh's death, James Murray served until what year, becoming the longest-serving U.S. senator in Montana history?
A. 1961.

Q. What senator secured congressional approval to build Canyon Ferry Dam, Yellowtail Dam, Hungry Horse Dam, and Libby Dam?
A. James Murray.

Q. Dave Manning of Hysham holds the record as the longest serving state legislator in the U.S.; how many years did he serve?
A. 52 years, from 1933 to 1985.

Q. What former Butte miner served as U.S. Senate majority leader for 15 years, longer than any other man in history?
A. Mike Mansfield.

Q. How much was the Blackfeet Indian Nation paid in 1896 for the property that now composes Glacier National Park?
A. $1.5 million, at $150,000 per year for 10 years.

Q. How much were the construction workers paid for working on Going-to-the-Sun Road in Glacier National Park?
A. 50 cents per hour for the work which was completed in 1932.

Q. How many workers died during the construction of the precarious Going-to-the Sun Road, which is 52 miles long?
A. Three: one lost his grip on a rope; one fell over a cliff; and one was hit by a falling rock. The employee turnover rate was 300 percent.

Q. The largest single meal ever served in Glacier was chili and hot dogs served to how many people on July 15, 1933, when Going-to-the-Sun Road was dedicated?
A. About 4,000.

Q. John D. Ryan, who created the Montana Power Company in order to provide cheap power to Butte mines, died in 1933 and was buried in a coffin made out of what?
A. Copper.

Q. In the 1930s, Butte mayor Charles Hauswirth skewered what public utility for taking one set of books to the IRS while taking a different set of books to rate hearings?
A. Montana Power Company.

Q. What dynamic U.S. senator who served from 1922 to 1946 once declared, "I've been accused of almost everything but timidity"?
A. Burton K. Wheeler.

Q. When Burton K. Wheeler was a young man passing through Montana, what unexpected circumstance forced him to stay in Butte and get a job?
A. He lost everything he had in a poker game.

Q. During the Great Depression, what was constructed using the single largest expenditure of federal money in the state?
A. Fort Peck Dam.

Q. How long did it take Senator Burton Wheeler to get FDR's approval to commit $75 million to build Fort Peck Dam?
A. 15 minutes.

Q. How long did it take to build Fort Peck Dam, the largest hydraulic earth-filled dam in the world, which backs up the fifth largest man-made reservoir and drains an area the size of Georgia?
A. Six years during the Depression. It was the largest project in FDR's New Deal program.

Q. How much was the average wage for those working on Fort Peck Dam?
A. 50 cents an hour for laborers and $1.20 an hour for skilled workers.

Q. Two weeks after the dam was completed, eight men were buried and the dam was ruined by a landslide of five million cubic yards of earth. How many bodies were never found?
A. Six. It took two more years to repair the damage to the dam.

Q. Where was Montana's German POW camp located during World War II?
A. In Laurel, in what is now Riverside Park.

Q. How many foreign men were detained at Fort Missoula during World War II?
A. 1,200 Italians and 650 Japanese-Americans.

Q. In 1954 the largest turnout of spectators in Missoula's history, estimated at 30,000, showed up to see President Dwight Eisenhower dedicate what?
A. The U.S. Forest Service's Smokejumper Center.

Q. Of the 16 smokejumpers who parachuted into Mann Gulch near Helena on August 9, 1949, to fight a small fire, how many survived after winds whipped the flames into a conflagration?
A. Three.

Q. When a flash flood destroyed a train trestle over Custer Creek on June 19, 1938, killing 49 of the 140 people on the next train, how far down the Yellowstone River were some of the bodies carried?
A. 130 miles to Sidney. It was Montana's worst railroad disaster.

Q. In June of 1964 when 16 inches of rain fell on country already waterlogged from melting winter snowpack, how many people died in the resulting floods?
A. 31, all of them on the remote Blackfeet Indian Reservation.

Q. How many Native Americans currently live in Montana?
A. About 50,000, or six percent of the population.

Q. How does Montana rank among states in percentage of Native American population?
A. Fifth, following Alaska, New Mexico, South Dakota, and Oklahoma.

Q. How many principal tribes inhabit the state's seven reservations?
A. 11: Blackfeet, Chippewa, Cree, Crow, Northern Cheyenne, Assiniboine, Sioux, Gros Ventre, Salish, Kootenai, and Little Shell.

Q. What's the largest tribe in the state?
A. Blackfeet, with about 8,500 living on or near the reservation.

Q. Who was the only member of Congress to vote against entering both World Wars?
A. Jeannette Rankin.

Q. What retired Montana representative led 5,000 women on a peace march in Washington, D.C., in June of 1970, on her 90th birthday?
A. Jeannette Rankin.

Q. How old was Joseph Toole, Montana's youngest governor, when he first took office in 1901?
A. 38.

Q. What happened to Governor Donald Nutter in 1962, only a year after he was elected?
A. He and five others died in a plane crash when winds tore a wing off his plane.

Q. How many telephone poles were snapped off by the same winds that doomed Governor's Nutter plane?
A. 66.

Q. What governor won affection for listing his home phone number in the directory and answering when it rang?
A. Ted Schwinden, 1981-1989.

Q. In 1995 what Montanan, now on the *Forbes* list of the richest Americans, received the Horatio Alger Award, given to people who have overcome adversity to achieve success?
A. Dennis Washington, who rose from poverty and started his own highway construction business in 1964. *Forbes* estimates Washington's net worth at $1.8 billion, which ranks him 236 on the list of the world's 500 richest people.

Q. How many states besides Montana have no general sales tax?
A. Four: Alaska, Delaware, New Hampshire, and Oregon.

Q. What was Montana's growth rate in 2000?
A. 0.2 percent, compared to the national average of 1.2 percent and that of Nevada (the fastest growing western state) at 5.4 percent.

History Word Search

```
R K R A L C D N A S I W E L L L Y
Q H E N R Y P L U M M E R O T N R
J T R J W G N I N N A M T S K A R
D P C K D Z R T H T T I R R I A F
C R U S E L E K Q K P E F L T E L
T H S P T Y P B L A N X R A N W S
Z E T R M T P D C I D O O Q E A R
K K E J O K O X M E A B T H E J E
S C R F Z T C M P D M C A O K A P
P E I Z K N C R O A L N F M O C M
A P L N W C E E E N A H Z E R A U
U T T X D S A T P C T X R S A S J
L R V B S I S L O S L A Y T S N E
D O W I R D A N B Z O N N E B L K
I F O R C Z D N K L T R L A A M O
N N W C Q A Y K S Q M T P D M M M
G R L I N D B E R G H D J R P C S
```

Answers on page 153

Absarokee	Lewis and Clark	Indians	Sacajawea
Steamboat	prospector	Custer	Henry Plummer
Cruse	copper	Spaulding	miners
Montana	capitol	Anaconda	Fort Peck
homestead	Lindbergh	Manning	railroad
depression	smokejumpers	Blackfeet	

ARTS & LITERATURE

Q. Having created posters, postcards, refrigerator magnets, and even painted buses in Japan, what Montana artist is known as the "Andy Warhol of Montana"?
A. Monte Dolack.

Q. The work of what Livingston artist has been called "a cross between Monet's impressionism and Gary Larson's 'Far Side' cartoon"?
A. Parks Reece, with such works as "Bisontennial", "Poultrygeist", and "The Rut Race".

Q. What is the name of the classical guitarist whose songs are inspired by and often named after Montana's rivers and mountains?
A. Stuart Weber.

Q. Who are the filmmaking brothers from Billings who made *Red Rock West* and *The Last Seduction*?
A. John and Rick Dahl.

Q. Detective writer Dashiell Hammett used what city as his model for the town of "Poisonville" in his novel *Red Harvest*?
A. Butte.

Q. A life-size Wells Fargo stagecoach drawn by a team of six horses created by Bill Dow of Billings appeared in Lewistown in the summer of 2001 sculpted from what medium?
A. Sand and Elmer's Guide.

Q. What explorers did Bill Dow sculpt in Lewistown in 2000 using 12 tons of sand?
A. "Lewis Sand Clark."

Q. What medium is used to create sculpture in a roadside art contest between Windham and Hobson each summer?
A. Hay bales in the "What the Hay" contest.

Q. What was the "white man's name" chosen by the Assiniboine artist whose "real" name was Fire Bear?
A. William Standing.

Q. The Archie Bray Foundation for the Ceramic Arts in Helena, a world-renowned retreat for potters, was originally the site of what business?
A. The Western Clay Manufacturing Company and Brickyard.

Q. What artist was painter Joseph H. Sharp referring to when he exclaimed, "She paints like a man!"?
A. Fra Dana, who lived on a ranch near Wyola.

Q. How much did the Charlie Russell watercolor *A Disputed Trail* sell for at auction in 2001?
A. $2.4 million.

Q. Why did the Montana Club in Helena have to sell the Charlie Russell painting it had commissioned to the Montana Historical Society?
A. The appraised value of $250,000 caused such high insurance premiums it depleted the club treasury.

Q. How many works of art did Charlie Russell create?
A. About 4,000, ranging from sketches, drawings, and paintings to sculpture.

Q. What Montana town ranked 59th in author John Vilani's survey of the "100 Best Small Art Towns in America"?
A. Helena.

Q. What tiny Montana town, population 300, is home of the prestigious Montana Artists Refuge?
A. Basin, south of Helena.

Q. In a survey by the Montana Historical Society in 2001, what book ranked number one as the best book about Montana?
A. *This House of Sky* by Ivan Doig, his memoirs of growing up near White Sulphur Springs.

Q. What book, which had previously held the top spot in a similar survey done in 1981, fell to number two?
A. *Montana: High, Wide, and Handsome* by Joseph Kinsey Howard.

Q. What prospector, one of the first to discover gold in Montana, wrote a book of his experiences from the diaries he kept?
A. Granville Stuart wrote *Forty Years on the Frontier as Seen in the Journals and Reminiscences of Granville Stuart.*

Q. What popular book was written by Mildred Walker in 1944 about the life of a girl growing up on a central Montana farm?
A. *Winter Wheat.*

Q. In 1990 what cowboy poet was the first to receive the National Endowment for the Arts' National Heritage Award?
A. Wally McRae.

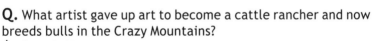

Q. What is Wally McRae's day job?
A. He's a third-generation Montana rancher.

Q. What artist gave up art to become a cattle rancher and now breeds bulls in the Crazy Mountains?
A. Dennis Voss.

Q. After becoming disillusioned with ranching, what Montana author turned to writing?
A. William Kittredge, author of *Who Owns the West?* and *Hole in the Sky.*

Q. William Kittredge and Annick Smith edited what 1,000-page book on Montana literature in 1992?
A. *The Last Best Place: A Montana Anthology.*

Q. What English professor at the University of Montana wrote a 1999 novel called *Shorty Harris, or The Price of Gold* about a prospector who finds gold, gives it all away, and dies broke?
A. William W. Bevis.

Q. How old is the rock art on the walls of Pictograph Cave near Billings?
A. Around 4,500 years old.

Q. What's the difference between a petroglyph and a pictograph?
A. Pictographs are painted on stone; petroglyphs are etched or carved into stone.

Q. How many artifacts have been recovered at Pictograph Cave State Park?
A. More than 30,000.

Q. While early Native American artists used natural substances to color their paints, such as ochre for yellow and charcoal for black, what did they use to make the color green?
A. Dried duck dung.

Q. When was the Indian Arts and Crafts Act passed, making it illegal to sell unauthenticated items claiming to be Indian art?
A. 1990.

Q. A. B. Guthrie, Jr., won the Pulitzer Prize for fiction in 1950 for what book?
A. *The Way West.*

Q. What Virginia City newspaper editor wrote a book in the 1860s called *Vigilantes of Montana* in which he defended the actions of the vigilantes?
A. Thomas Dimsdale, who is suspected of having been a vigilante himself.

Q. What famous comic book artist (E. C. Comics) and longtime editor of *MAD* magazine now resides in Livingston?
A. Al Feldstein.

Q. How many private art galleries across the state sell the work of Montana artists?
A. About 287.

Q. Montana's first and oldest library, founded in 1868, is in what city?
A. Helena— the Lewis and Clark County Library.

Q. The 79 tax-supported libraries in the state circulate an average of how many books per resident per year?
A. 5.9 books.

Q. The state contains how many museums?
A. Approximately 230.

Q. Montana has how many newspapers?
A. 85, including 11 dailies.

Q. In what town would you find *The Madisonian,* the state's oldest continuously published newspaper, started in 1873?
A. Virginia City.

Q. Of the 896 public K-12 schools in the state, how many have only one teacher, fewer than 18 students, and could be considered to be one-room schoolhouses?
A. 76.

Q. What county has the greatest number of one-room schoolhouses, with eight?
A. Garfield, followed by Custer County with seven.

Q. How many states have a lower average salary for elementary school teachers than the $33,000 Montana teachers earned in 2001?
A. Only two: North Dakota and South Dakota.

Q. What percent of Montanans over the age of 25 graduated from high school?
A. 89.6 percent, ranking the state 11th in the nation.

Q. What percent of people over 25 years old graduated from college?
A. 24.4 percent, ranking the state 18th in the nation.

Q. What town is home to Dull Knife College, named after a Cheyenne chief who urged his people to pursue education?
A. Lame Deer.

Q. How many Fulbright Scholars have come from University of Montana?
A. 39.

Q. How many Rhodes Scholars have come out of University of Montana?
A. 28, making it fourth in the nation for per capita number of students selected.

Q. How many Pulitzer Prize winners have come out of University of Montana's school of journalism?
A. Seven.

Q. What poet taught creative writing at University of Montana for 18 years, won a Guggenheim Fellowship, published numerous volumes of poetry, and died in 1982?
A. Richard Hugo.

Q. Author Richard Ford, who maintains a household in Montana, won a Pulitzer Prize in 1996 for what novel?
A. *Independence Day*, which was the first novel to win both the Pulitzer and the PEN/Faulkner Award.

Q. The former huge holding tanks of the city water treatment plant in what eastern Montana town now contain an art center?
A. Miles City.

Q. *Today I Baled Some Hay to Feed the Sheep the Coyotes Eat*, which takes a humorous and realistic look at sheep ranching, was written and illustrated by what Grass Range artist, author, and rancher?
A. Bill Stockton.

Q. Bill Stockton, who claims he doesn't know whether he is "an artist who ranches or a rancher who arts" commonly uses what unusual artistic medium in his paintings?
A. A cattle marker, a huge chalky crayon used to mark livestock.

Q. Evelyn Cameron, an upper-class English woman who came to Terry in the late 1800s, became a photographer in an effort to support herself after what business failed?
A. Raising polo ponies on a ranch with her husband.

Q. Officials in Miles City threatened to arrest Evelyn Cameron around the turn of the century for committing what crime?
A. Wearing an indecent skirt that was divided up the middle to allow her to ride a horse astride instead of sidesaddle.

Q. Christened with the name Joseph Ernest Nephtali Dufault, the Western writer and artist who wrote and illustrated 23 books is better known by what name?
A. Will James, who had a ranch on Pryor Creek and a home in Billings.

Q. What Will James sketch portrays a cowboy calmly standing in the doorway of his sod cabin while, unbeknownst to him, a grizzly stands on the roof?
A. *Ignorance Is Bliss.*

Q. What Bozeman artist is known for sculpting mobiles out of large rocks, which are so perfectly balanced they effortlessly spin in the slightest breeze?
A. Zak Zakovi.

Q. Kidnapped by Indians, what artist drew their portraits so realistically as they discussed how to kill him that the amazed captors released him?
A. Edgar S. Paxson.

Q. Backdrops painted a century ago by the famous muralist Edgar S. Paxson were returned to what theater in 1998, where they now decorate the walls?
A. Philipsburg Opera House.

Q. What artist was Charlie Russell referring to when he said, "His brush told stories that people like to read"?
A. Edgar S. Paxson.

Q. The most famous of Edgar S. Paxson's nearly 2,000 paintings depicts what battle?
A. Custer's Last Stand.

Q. What factor hindered Paxson's progress as he labored for eight years in Butte to complete his masterpiece depicting Custer's Last Stand?
A. The sulfurous smoke from the nearby smelter obscured the light he needed to paint.

Q. What well-known Montana author wrote in his book *Some Horses,* "If a horse were a Ford, the species would vanish beneath lawsuits engendered by consumer-protection laws"?
A. Tom McGuane.

Q. What was the first big break in Charlie Russell's career that helped boost him out of obscurity?
A. He married Nancy Cooper, who had the guts to sell his paintings for what they were truly worth.

Q. What other factor skyrocketed Charlie Russell to fame?
A. A contract with Brown and Bigelow Calendar Company that put his art in front of millions.

Q. Performance artist Kristi Hager staged what "art action" at Butte's Berkeley Pit in July 2000 to draw attention to the rising level of toxic water?
A. A gathering of 150 hula dancers performed at the lip of the pit to the song "Cool Water."

Q. What artist sculpted the bronze statue of Old Shep, a faithful dog at Fort Benton who waited more than five years at the train station for the return of his dead master?
A. Bob Scriver.

Q. Following his retirement from the auto repair business at age seventy, what Missoula man became a sculptor?
A. E. W. Riley.

Q. Artist and Montana resident Robert DeWeese served as an inspiration for what book written by Robert Pirsig?
A. *Zen and the Art of Motorcycle Maintenance.*

Q. From what medium does Tina DeWeese, daughter of Robert DeWeese, compose her sculptures?
A. Wire.

Q. How old was Gennie DeWeese, wife of Robert DeWeese, when she accepted the Governor's Award for Excellence in the Arts in 1995 on behalf of herself and her deceased husband?
A. 75.

Q. Josh DeWeese, son of artist Robert DeWeese, is the director of what artistic foundation in Helena?
A. Archie Bray Foundation for the Ceramic Arts.

Q. In what book did author Teddy Blue Abbott give a recipe for Indian whiskey, which included Missouri River water, alcohol, strychnine, tobacco, soap, pepper, and sagebrush?
A. *We Pointed Them North: Recollections of a Cowpuncher.*

Q. What author of *The Longest Silence: A Life in Fishing* once stated, "When the trout are gone, smash the state"?
A. Tom McGuane.

Q. How many murals were painted on the walls and ceiling of the St. Ignatius Mission church by Brother Joseph Carignano, a cook at the school with no art training?
A. 58.

Q. What Missoula artist is known for his whimsical depictions of wild animals wreaking havoc in human homes?
A. Monte Dolack.

Q. What watercolor artist married to Monte Dolack is known for her portrayals of intimate moments in nature?
A. Mary Beth Percival.

Q. What Montana potter, whose bulbous and oddly shaped pots feature drawings of horses and naked women, commands prices of $25,000 and up for his vessels?
A. Rudy Autio of Missoula.

Q. Chris Autio, son of ceramic artist Rudy Autio, works in what medium?
A. Photography and video.

Q. Lela Autio, wife of ceramic artist Rudy Autio, works in what medium?
A. Assemblages of plastic pieces and enamel in a 3-D style of art.

Q. What unusual medium does Blackfeet artist Jay Laber use to build his life-size sculptures?
A. Rusted abandoned car parts.

Q. What Missoula artist has been likened to a modern Andrew Wyeth?
A. Stephanie Frostad.

Q. What artist and cofounder of the Archie Bray Foundation was credited with having transformed traditional conservative ceramics into the art of abstract expressionistic sculpture?
A. Peter Voulkos.

Q. When ceramic artist Peter Voulkos informed his Greek mother he was going to be a potter, what was her response?
A. "What! Make pots and pans! I thought you gonna be an artist!"

Q. Linda McCray's artwork focuses on what subject?
A. Railroad scenes of Montana and North America.

Q. What artist has been called a "poet of dusk and of daybreak" for his dramatic lighting of Montana landscapes?
A. Dale Livezey.

Q. The building housing the Paris Gibson Museum of Art in Great Falls was originally what?
A. Central High School.

Q. Emerson Cultural Center in Bozeman, housing many kinds of galleries and studios, is in a building formerly used as what?
A. An elementary school.

Q. What Helena sculptor was the first American artist invited to give a solo exhibit at the Hermitage Museum in St. Petersburg, Russia, the world's largest art museum?
A. Tim Holmes.

Q. The 2001 book *Symphony in the Brain,* which explores using neurofeedback to control seizures, is the work of what Helena author?
A. Jim Robbins.

Q. The 26-room, four-floor Arts Chateau in Butte was originally the French-style mansion of whom?
A. Charles Walker Clark, son of copper king W. A. Clark, once the richest man on earth.

Q. Photographer F. Jay Haynes became famous in the late 1800s for spending 32 years photographing what subject?
A. Yellowstone National Park.

Q. When F. Jay Haynes rode through Montana photographing the landscape and the people, where was his darkroom located?
A. In a customized railroad car.

Q. In 1927 what writer and religious leader started his writing career as joke editor on the Helena High School Newspaper?
A. L. Ron Hubbard, author of *Dianetics* and founder of Scientology.

Q. The state's two statues in the National Statuary Hall of the U.S. Capitol represent what Montanans?
A. Congresswoman Jeannette Rankin and artist Charlie Russell.

Q. Sculptor-in-bronze John B. Weaver, who created the statue of Charlie Russell in the U.S. Capitol, made what statue in downtown Helena?
A. *The Bullwhacker,* a 12-foot cowpoke with a really big whip.

Q. What author of *A River Runs Through It* became well known as a writer only after he had retired from being a college professor?
A. Norman Maclean, who was 70 when he wrote the book.

Q. How many other books did Norman Maclean write in his lifetime?
A. Just one, *Young Men and Fire,* which was published after his death.

Q. Norman Maclean's book *Young Men and Fire* was an account of what forest fire near Helena that killed 13 smokejumpers?
A. Mann Gulch.

Q. When Mark Twain wrote the book *Following the Equator* about his yearlong speaking tour in 1895, how much space did he give to the five engagements he had in Montana?
A. A single sentence, complaining about the heat and the forest fire smoke.

Q. The statue of what national figure in front of the Helena courthouse is occasionally decked out in such regalia as coonskin caps, horse blankets, and grass skirts?
A. George Washington.

Q. When sculptor Edmund Carns built a 62-foot-tall elk made of copper to celebrate the Butte Elks Lodge convention in 1916, how long did it straddle Broadway and Main before being torn down and re-smelted?
A. Less than a month.

Q. What noted Helena artist was one of the first to pioneer polymer clays as an artistic medium, at a time when polymer clay was still considered merely a child's play thing?
A. Margaret Regan.

Q. Ernest Hemingway described what Montana city in *For Whom the Bell Tolls?*
A. Missoula.

Q. What Helena artist and gallery owner has paintings and prints residing in collections on all seven continents, including the Amundsen-Scott Research Center in Antarctica?
A. Doug Turman.

Q. Photographer Margaret Bourke-White took the photo of what man-made Montana landmark that appeared in the first issue of *Life* magazine in 1936?
A. Fort Peck Dam.

Q. What author and artist, born in Billings, created the comic strips *Rick O'Shay, Latigo,* and *Grass Roots?*
A. Stan Lynde.

Q. The abandoned Northern Pacific Depot in Livingston now houses what?
A. The Depot Center Museum.

Q. What Havre artist has used photography to preserve images of the Rocky Boy's Indian Reservation?
A. John Well-Off-Man.

Q. What Helena artist is known for her bronze sculptures depicting nostalgic moments of an era gone by?
A. Becky Eiker.

Q. Author Tom McGuane in the 1994 book *Nothing But Blue Skies* writes about the happenings of a town named Deadrock, a humorous poke at what city?
A. Livingston ("living-stone") where he lived.

Q. What outdoor humor writer and author of such books as *Pecked to Death by Ducks* and *A Wolverine Is Eating My Leg* is a long-time resident of Livingston?
A. Tim Cahill.

Q. What outdoor writer got his start by play-ing dead in order to attract buzzards so he could write an article about them, which was pub-lished in the *San Francisco Examiner?*
A. Tim Cahill.

Q. What Livingston writer was a founding editor of *Outside* Magazine?
A. Tim Cahill.

Q. Charlie Russell wrote and illustrated what collection of short stories?
A. *Trails Plowed Under: Stories of the Old West.*

Q. What artist, born in Boulder, was given the name *Moquea Stumik* meaning "man about size of wolf with heart big as buf-falo bull" by the Blackfeet, whom he often painted?
A. Irvin "Shorty" Shope.

Q. Writer Frank Bird Linderman, who wrote extensively about Indians, wrote 12 of his 13 books from his home on what Mon-tana lake?
A. Flathead Lake, where he had a home at Goosehead Bay.

Q. What Livingston artist, who has had more than 300 shows, is also the author of such books as *The Anglers Coast* and *Dark Waters?*
A. Russell Chatham.

Q. What is the most photographed building in Meagher County?
A. The long abandoned, weather-beaten Catholic church on the hill in Ringling, currently being restored.

Q. What Whitefish writer, now deceased, wrote *The Bedside Book of Bastards* with R. T. Turner in 1973?
A. Dorothy Johnson.

Q. A town on the Flathead Indian Reservation was named after what man who wrote a history of the Flathead Indians?
A. Major Peter Ronan, who was superintendent of the reservation in 1885.

Q. What writer wrote, "Montana is a remote hinterland about as well known to the average eastern seaboard citizen as East or West Africa...."?
A. Joseph Kinsey Howard in his 1943 book *Montana: High, Wide, and Handsome.*

Q. What writer said of Montana, "For other states I have admiration, respect, recognition, even some affection, but with Montana it is love, and it's difficult to analyze love when you're in it"?
A. John Steinbeck.

Q. In 1832 the first steamboat to reach Fort Union near the Montana border carried what portrayer of Indian culture as a passenger?
A. George Catlin.

Q. What prompted George Catlin's interest in Indian culture?
A. His mother at the age of seven was kidnapped by the Iroquois.

Q. How old was Herbert Kirk in 1993 when he was awarded a Bachelor of Arts degree from Montana State University, becoming the oldest graduate in the history of the school?
A. 97.

Q. Where is the oldest continuously used school building in the state, built in the 1880s?
A. Trinity School in Canyon Creek, which now has six students.

Q. Lucia Darling, niece of the first territorial governor Sidney Edgerton, set up the territory's first school in Bannack and later wrote her memoirs in what book?
A. *Crossing the Plains,* about her trip from Ohio to Montana in 1863.

Q. What Montana artist, sculptor, and printmaker also drilled one of the state's first oil wells?
A. Branson Stevenson.

Q. Blackfeet newspaper columnist John Tatsey collected some of his columns written in the 1950s and 1960s into a book entitled what?
A. The Black Moccasin.

Q. What newspaper won a Pulitzer Prize for covering the devastating floods of 1964, becoming the first in the state to win the prize?
A. *The Hungry Horse News* edited by Mel Ruder.

Q. Eric Newhouse of the *Great Falls Tribune* won a Pulitzer Prize in 2000 for his 12-part series on what topic?
A. Alcohol and alcoholism.

Q. What Helena artist painted the murals at the Agriculture Museum in Fort Benton?
A. Bob Morgan.

Q. Lester Thorow, economist and best-selling author, was born in what town?
A. Livingston.

Q. In 1960 what historian, who promoted the historical markers across the state, also wrote a historical account of the cattle industry entitled *Free Grass to Fences?*
A. Bob Fletcher.

Q. The account of what faithful dog was sold to railroad passengers to raise funds for the Montana School for the Deaf and Blind?
A. Old Shep, who waited for more than five years at the Fort Benton rail depot for his dead master to return.

Q. What sculptor, painter, and carver became deaf as a child from scarlet fever?
A. John L. Clarke, born in Highwood in 1881.

Q. What name did the Blackfeet bestow upon artist John L. Clarke?
A. *Catapuis,* meaning "man-who-talks-not."

Q. What was unusual about Blackfeet artist Ernie Pepion?
A. He did his paintings from a wheelchair after a car accident left him a quadriplegic for the final 33 years of his life. He died in 2005 at the age of 61.

Q. In 1929 Montana native Taylor Gordon, who sang all over the world and appeared in a number of movies in the 1930s, wrote his autobiography entitled what?
A. *Born to Be.*

Q. What physical feature made Taylor Gordon stand out among all the residents of his hometown of White Sulphur Springs?
A. His family was the only black family in town.

Q. What was Gordon's nickname, bestowed upon him by his friends in White Sulphur Springs?
A. "Snowball."

Q. Tenor Taylor Gordon, who toured vaudeville stages of the United States, as well as the concert halls of Europe, was once a chauffeur for what ex-circus man who fostered his singing talent?
A. John Ringling, founder of the town of Ringling near White Sulpher Springs.

Q. What artist created a large mural depicting the four seasons of neighbor helping neighbor for the Missoula Food Bank?
A. Stephanie Frostad.

Q. What book won the American Book Award and the *Los Angeles Times* Book Prize for Native American writer James Welch?
A. *Fools Crow*, published in 1986.

Q. What Missoula author was knighted by the French government for his contribution to the arts and letters?
A. James Welch, who died in 2003.

Q. Grace Stone Coates, who won critical acclaim in 1931 for her first novel *Black Cherries*, wrote how many other novels?
A. None, though she wrote two volumes of poetry.

Q. Martinsdale writer Lee Rostad wrote the life story of what other Martinsdale writer in her book *Honey Wine and Hunger Root*?
A. Grace Stone Coates.

Q. Lee Rostad's book *Fourteen Cents and Seven Green Apples* tells the story of what wealthy Martinsdale sheep rancher?
A. Charles Bair.

Q. What historian and author of *Montana: An Uncommon Land* once proclaimed, "If America is running out of anything, it is Montana"?
A. K. Ross Toole.

Q. What historian and writer founded *Montana, the Magazine of Western History*?
A. K. Ross Toole.

Q. The International Fly Fishing Center, a museum dedicated to fishing, is in what town?
A. Livingston.

Q. Mary MacLane in 1902 at the age of nineteen published *The Story of Mary MacLane* which became an overnight sensation, was describing her life in what rollicking town?
A. Butte.

Q. Gary Svee wrote the book *Spirit Wolf*, winner of the 1996 Golden Spur Award, about the search for the last wolf in what southern Montana mountain range?
A. The Pryors.

Q. What counter-culture poet and writer, author of *Trout Fishing in America*, owned property in Montana?
A. Richard Brautigan.

Q. Lauri Gano portrays the scenic landscapes around her Sweet Grass County ranch using what medium?
A. Fibers, woven to make intricate tapestries that look like oil paintings.

Q. What photographer published her black-and-white photos of Montana in a 1996 collection called *The Back of Beyond: The Ranching West*?
A. Barbara Van Cleve.

Q. In Paul Winter's Grammy Award-winning album *Prayer for the Wild Things*, how many animal sounds can be heard, many of them recorded in Glacier National Park?
A. 27, each listed as members of the band.

Q. In what 1996 mystery by Montana author William Hjortsberg does the killer re-create scenes from the pages of Edgar Allen Poe while Arthur Conan Doyle and Harry Houdini work to catch him?
A. *Nevermore.*

Q. John Frohnmayer of Bozeman was once the controversial chairman of the National Endowment for the Arts and wrote what books about the experience?
A. *Leaving Town Alive: Confessions of an Arts Warrior.*

Q. The building in downtown Helena that once housed Montana Powder and Equipment— the place to go for all your dynamite needs—now houses what?
A. Holter Museum of Art.

Q. In what city would you find the MonDak Heritage Center, one of the state's most remote art centers, where Christmas each year celebrates a different ethnic group?
A. Sidney, where the nearest art center is 128 miles away.

Q. *Our Lady of the Rockies*, a 90-foot statue of the Madonna, stands on top of a ridge high above what town?
A. Butte.

Q. Where would you find a 27-foot tall concrete penguin standing on a base that reads "Coldest Spot in the Nation"?
A. Cut Bank.

Q. Where would you find the bison that served as the model for the buffalo nickel and the 1901 ten-dollar bill?
A. The Museum of Northern Plains in Fort Benton.

Q. Where was that bison shot?
A. Near the Musselshell River in 1886— it was stuffed and displayed at the Smithsonian Institution for years.

Q. Carl Mehmke collects what kind of antique farm implements at his museum near Great Falls?
A. Antique tractors (more than a 100 of them) and steam engines.

Q. What town museum displays the homestead cabin of John "Liver-Eating" Johnston, the mountain man the movie *Jeremiah Johnson* was based on?
A. The Carbon County Museum in Red Lodge.

Q. The Gideons, who are famous for placing Bibles in hotel rooms, placed their first Bibles in their first hotel in 1908, in what town?
A. Superior, at the Superior Hotel.

Q. How many bronze sculptures of everything from Jesus Christ to a dog, did Browning artist Bob Scriver leave behind when he died in 1999?
A. More than 1,000.

Q. Montana resident Mildred Walker wrote what novel, which was later turned into a Broadway play and then a movie?
A. *The Southwest Corner.*

Q. In what northwestern town has the county jail been trans-formed into a museum?
A. Thompson Falls, site of the Old Jail Museum.

Q. What historian and author of eight books about Montana's past received the 1999 H. G. Merriam Award for distinguished contributions to Montana literature?
A. Mike Malone.

Q. Who donated the money to build a twice-life-size statue of cattle baron Pierre Wibaux to stand over the town of Wibaux?
A. Pierre Wibaux himself, who also petitioned for the town name to be changed from Mingusville to Wibaux (pronounced WE-beau).

Q. Photographer Bruce Selyem of Bozeman specializes in photos of what type of obsolete structures?
A. Grain elevators—he started the Country Grain Elevator Historical Society.

Q. The 1984 book by Steve Smith *The Years and the Wind and the Rain* was a biography of what Montana writer, who died mere weeks after it was published?
A. Dorothy M. Johnson.

Q. Middle school teacher Jim Schulz of Helena won what award in 2001?
A. The Disney American Teacher Award for being one of the nation's most outstanding middle school science teachers.

Q. What author married a Nez Perce woman, accompanied the tribe on their fighting flight across the state, mourned her when she died, and wrote a book called *Tough Trip Through Paradise* to describe the war from his point of view?
A. Andrew Garcia.

Q. What writer from New York was orphaned at 13, moved west to live with his uncle, lived with the Blackfeet for more than a decade, married into the tribe, and wrote a book called *My Life as an Indian* published in 1907 and still in print?
A. James Willard Schultz.

Q. What online magazine launched by George Everett in 1999 focuses exclusively on unusual items of Butte history?
A. *Only in Butte.*

Q. The American Computer Museum, one of the most comprehensive displays on the history of the information age, is in what city?
A. Bozeman.

Q. What eastern Montana museum displays a petrified oyster?
A. The Pierre Wibaux Museum in Wibaux.

Q. What mid-Montana museum displays not only a stagecoach that has bullet holes sustained during a holdup but also fossilized gizzard stones of a dinosaur?
A. Upper Musselshell Museum in Harlowton.

Q. In what town would you find on display the mummified clubfoot of "Clubfoot George" who was hanged by vigilantes in 1863?
A. Virginia City. His foot was exhumed to prove they'd hung the right guy.

Q. What artist created murals for the state capitol in Helena as well as the courthouse in Missoula?
A. Edgar S. Paxson.

Q. The longest interior painting in Montana, a mural four feet tall and 74 feet long painted by Bob Southland, depicts the history of what county?
A. Sheridan, on display at the Sheridan County Museum near Plentywood.

Q. What artistic project ruined the eyesight of Olaf Carl Seltzer so that he was afterwards only able to paint in bright light?
A. A series of 100 miniatures depicting Montana history, painted with a magnifying glass.

Q. At the annual Outhouse Olympics in Kentucky, author Bob Ross of Bozeman received what unusual award in 1998?
A. The Crescent Moon Award "for promoting and preserving outhouses with great dignity." His four *Muddled Meanderings* books are about outhouses.

Q. What Montana adventure writer set a world record by driving from Tierra del Fuego, Chili, to Prudhoe Bay, Alaska, in 23 days, documenting the journey in a book called *Road Fever*?
A. Tim Cahill.

Q. The town of Rudyard is named after what poet?
A. Rudyard Kipling, who came through the area in 1889.

Q. When photographer L. A. Huffman of Miles City traveled around documenting the cowboys and Indians of the frontier West in the 1880s, how much did his handmade camera weigh?
A. 50 pounds.

Q. When various sculptors were asked to create 29 statues for the St. Helena Cathedral depicting people who had helped mankind, they produced statues of Columbus, Pasteur, Gutenberg, Dante, Copernicus, Joan of Arc, Michelangelo, and various saints. Who did artist Monsignor John Tougas sculpt?
A. His mom, Charlotte.

Q. What artist produced around 200 portraits of the Indians who fought Custer at the Battle of the Little Big Horn?
A. J. H. Sharp.

Q. What author penned her Montana memories in a book published in 2001 called *All But the Waltz*?
A. Mary Clearman Blew.

Q. Before he was an artist and professor of art of University of Montana, what was Walter Hook's totally unrelated job?
A. Working for the Atomic Energy Commission.

Q. Western writer Richard S. Wheeler, winner of three Spur Awards, was once a reporter in what town?
A. Billings.

Q. Charlie Russell had an art studio behind his home in Great Falls that was constructed of what material?
A. Telephone poles.

Q. What was the middle name of artist Charlie M. Russell?
A. Marion.

Q. What man founded the first Audubon Society, edited *Forest and Stream* magazine, pushed for the formation of Glacier Park, founded the Boone and Crockett Club to advocate fair hunting practices, and now has a glacier in the park named after him?
A. George Bird Grinnell.

Q. What prompted George Bird Grinnell to found the Audubon Society?
A. The large number of dead birds appearing on women's hats.

Q. What caused the Grinnell Glacier in Glacier National Park to greatly accelerate the pace of its melting in 1980?
A. Ashfall from the eruption of Mt. Saint Helens fell on the glacier and absorbed sunlight and heat.

Q. How did sculptor Steve Thorstenson protest the widespread environmental contamination of his hometown of Libby?
A. Because Libby soil had been polluted by asbestos due to vermiculite mining, he covered some of his sculptures with vermiculite.

Q. What Missoula writer wrote a book called *Last Breath: The Limits of Adventure* in which he describes in excruciating detail what the final moments of life feel like for adventurers whose adventure has gone awry?
A. Peter Stark.

Art & Literature Word Scramble

1. YDUR IOUTA   ____ _____

2. RHCLAEI ERLUSSL   _____ _____

3. GNAIVIIR TCIY   _____ ____

4. RLDAFIGE YNTUCO   _____ _____

5. ORYHODT OJSNHON   _____ _____

6. ELEVYN MNOEACR   _____ _____

7. OBB RCRIVES   ___ _____

8. YRBEKELE IPT   _____ ___

9. RIITSP LWOF   _____ ____

10. OVNESILOILP   _____

11. HTE ATSL ESTB ALECP   ___ ____ ____ _____

12. RIOPHCTAGP EAVC STETA AKPR   _____ ____ _____ ____

13. EQMAOU ITSKUM   _____ _____

14. YAWLL CEMAR   _____ _____

15. TYOALR DNGROO   _____ _____

16. OFOLS WCOR   _____ ____

17. AMEL REDE   ____ ____

18. MOETN LDOAK   _____ _____

19. AGEDR PAXNO   _____ _____

20. OANMRN MCELAAN   _____ _____

Answers on page 153

Created with the help of Worksheets—www.Qualint.com

Q**uote**

Quest

Find the words every which way from this Mark Singer quote: "Cooke City has a winter population of a hundred self-selected souls - all of whom, it seems, are wedded to the proposition that the climate is ideal." *When all the clues have been circled, the remaining letters will form a secret message.*

cooke
city
winter
population
hundred
self
selected
souls
whom
seems
wedded
proposition
that
climate
ideal

```
P I N M O N W E D D E D T
N O A N A T H T E R S E C
O S P T S H R E H E E T L
I H E U I L N G L A S W I
T E K A L R U F E S T N M
I E O V E A I O M R H L A
S A O T E D T E S Y U M T
O F C O E R E I T C N O E
P H U A R S C I O H D H W
O O L R K A C N D N R W F
R D E T C E L E S I E S H
P I N W I N T E R G D W M
```

Quote Quest © 2005 by Janet Spencer

Solution

Hidden message:
"In Montana there's three things we are never late for: church, work and fishing." -Norman Maclean, "A River Runs Through It"

Want more Quote Quest?
Look for the Quote Quest puzzle book by Janet Spencer and Riverbend Publishing, coming soon, or contact Janet Spencer at Janet@TriviaQueen.com to reserve your copy today.

SPORTS &
LEISURE

Q. How many state parks are in Montana?
A. 43, totaling almost 28,000 acres.

Q. What is the largest state park?
A. Makoshika, a badlands area, with 8,834 acres.

Q. *Makoshika* is a Sioux word meaning what?
A. "Land of bad spirits."

Q. About how many people visit Makoshika State Park every year?
A. 40,000.

Q. About how many buzzards spend their summers in Makoshika State Park?
A. 60. They are also called turkey vultures.

Q. When is the annual "Buzzard Day" celebrated at Makoshika Park with fun runs, pancake breakfast, kite flying, nature walks, and folf tournament?
A. Second Saturday in June.

Q. Fossils of how many different species of dinosaurs have been found in Makoshika State Park?
A. 10, with the search continuing.

Q. What is the smallest state park?
A. Granite State Park, a single building in Granite, a ghost town near Philipsburg.

Q. What is the most frequently visited state park?
A. Cooney Reservoir south of Columbus with almost 200,000 visitors in 2000.

Q. What cave in western Montana is one of the largest lime-stone caverns in the northwest portion of the nation?
A. Lewis and Clark Caverns, the state's first state park, established in 1937.

Q. What is the most recent addition to the state park system, added in 2004?
A. Tower Rock on the Missouri River near Cascade.

Q. Where in Montana can you shoot a gun competitively from inside a house?
A. In Butte, at the Gun Club's Rocker Range, where you can shoot targets from the shelter of the Scheutzen house.

Q. What percentage of the adult male population of Montana buys a hunting license annually?
A. 41 percent, plus seven percent of women.

Q. What percentage of residents own fire-arms suitable for hunting?
A. 38.1 percent, a greater percentage than any other state.

Q. What percent of Montanans live in a household with at least one gun?
A. 57 percent. The only states with a higher percentage are Alaska (58%); South Dakota (59%); and Wyoming (60%).

Q. What state has the lowest percentage of people who live in a household with at least one gun?
A. Hawaii with 10 percent, followed by New Jersey, Massachusetts, Rhode Island, and Connecticut.

Q. How many homicides were there in Montana in the year 2002?
A. 16, compared to 2,395 in California the same year.

Q. How many states had fewer homicides than Montana in 2002?
A. Six: Wyoming (15); Maine (14); Vermont (13); New Hampshire (12); South Dakota (11); and North Dakota (5).

Q. What percentage of adult residents of both sexes buy a fishing license each year?
A. 34 percent.

Q. What percentage of people buying a fishing license are from out of state?
A. 42 percent.

Q. How many Fish, Wildlife and Parks game wardens patrol the state?
A. 92, each covering an area about the size of Delaware.

Q. What's the most common violation of fish and game laws?
A. Fishing without a license.

Q. With one person spending one day fishing counting as a single fishing day, how many fishing days are spent in Montana waters every year, according to Fish, Wildlife and Parks?
A. 3.2 million.

Q. What percentage of deer and pronghorn antelope are found on privately owned land?
A. 62 percent of mule deer, 68 percent of white-tailed deer, and 75 percent of pronghorn.

Q. What is the most commonly hunted big game animal?
A. Deer, with about 89,000 taken every year.

Q. What is the second most commonly hunted big game animal?
A. Elk and pronghorn tied, with about 20,000 each.

Q. Where was the nation's first designated snowmobile trail located?
A. Two Top, outside West Yellowstone.

Q. What town, with 150 inches of snow annually and 600 miles of groomed trails, bills itself as the "snowmobile capital of the world"?
A. West Yellowstone.

Q. Where is the official test site and promotional filming grounds of both Yamaha and Arctic Cat snowmobiles?
A. Cooke City, with an average annual snowfall of 205 inches.

Q. The TransMontana Ride is the state's longest snowmobile event, traveling how many miles?
A. 450 miles from Eureka to West Yellowstone.

Q. Who played center and offensive tackle for the University of Montana Grizzlies, the New York Jets, and the Atlanta Falcons?
A. Guy Bingham, now retired from football and living in Missoula.

Q. What Shelby-born athlete played forward-center for the San Antonio Spurs, the Milwaukee Bucks, the Utah Jazz, the Orlando Magic, the Chicago Bulls, and the Los Angeles Lakers?
A. Larry Krystkowiak, who averaged 12.7 points and 7.6 rebounds per game during 1988-89.

Q. What Montana-born professional football player wrote a number of books about sports, including *Instant Replay* in 1968 and *Distant Replay* in 1985?
A. Jerry Kramer.

Q. Who coached the Chicago Bulls beginning in 1989, leading them to six NBA world championships and getting himself voted NBA Coach of the Year in 1996?
A. Phil Jackson, born in Deer Lodge.

Q. Who began as a defensive tackle for the University of Montana Grizzlies and went on to play for the Chicago Bears, Minnesota Vikings, New Orleans Saints, Houston Oilers, and Atlanta Falcons?
A. Mike Tilleman of Chinook, whose NFL career spanned 1965-1976.

Q. What Norwegian athlete came to Montana State University on a skiing scholarship, became a place kicker for the Bobcats, and ended up in the Pro Football Hall of Fame in 1991?
A. Jan Stenerud.

Q. What annual 350-mile sled dog race starts near Lincoln and is considered one of the top five sled dogs races on earth?
A. The Race to the Sky.

Q. How old was Jessie Royer in 1994 when she became not only the youngest musher ever to win the Race to the Sky but also the first woman to win?
A. 17.

Q. About how many different pro rodeos are held throughout the state each year?
A. More than 25.

Q. How long does a bull rider need to stay on the bull to qualify in rodeo?
A. Eight seconds.

Q. For more than 80 years, what town has hosted the Wild Horse Stampede, which has been called "the granddaddy of Montana rodeos"?
A. Wolf Point.

Q. Where is the biggest Native American rodeo in the state, held every August, with more than 40,000 tickets typically sold?
A. The Crow Fair, held near Crow Agency.

Q. How many species of fish are in the state?
A. 90, of which 56 are native.

Q. How many of those 90 species are classified as game fish?
A. 31.

Q. What species of game fish is most often found on the end of a fishing line?
A. Rainbow trout.

Q. How many fish hatcheries are in the state?
A. Nine, stocking 42.5 million fish, of which 95 percent go into lakes and reservoirs.

Q. In what year was whirling disease, a fatal parasitic infection of trout and salmon, first found in the state's rivers?
A. 1994, in the upper Madison River.

Q. In 1999, how many sites tested positive for whirling disease?
A. 83.

Q. In 2004, how many sites tested positive for whirling disease?
A. 137.

Q. How is whirling disease spread?
A. By transplanting live fish or dead fish parts from infected waters into clean streams.

Q. How many public fishing access sites does the Department of Fish, Wildlife and Parks administer?
A. About 320.

Q. Spring Meadow Lake State Recreation Area in Helena used to be the site of what kind of business?
A. A gravel pit—then workers struck water and now it is a lake.

Q. What town in Montana changed its name to Joe for the duration of the 1993 football season as a publicity stunt to honor NFL quarterback Joe Montana?
A. Ismay, which had a population of 20 at the time. Joe Montana never visited Joe, Montana.

Q. The only pitcher to hit a grand slam in the history of the World Series, what baseball player started his pitching career in Billings?
A. Dave McNally of the Baltimore Orioles, who hit his grand slam in 1970. Dave died in Billings in 2002.

Q. What small town hired baseball players from the blacklisted Chicago Black Sox in order to help them beat the Plentywood team in 1925?
A. Scobey. (Scobey won.)

Q. What baseball team has won 24 state championships and played in four American Legion World Series playoffs?
A. The Billings American Legion team.

Q. How many downhill ski areas are in the state?
A. 16, with a combined area of 14,000 thousand acres of skiing and 548 downhill runs.

Q. How long would it take to give a lift to the entire population of Montana in the state's 65 ski lifts?
A. About 13 hours at maximum capacity of 72,000 people per hour.

Q. What was the first commercial ski resort to open in the state?
A. Big Mountain near Whitefish, opened in 1947.

Q. The most vertical feet of skiing in the nation are found in what ski area?
A. Big Sky, with 4,180 feet.

Q. Who threw the discus for MSU and later won America's first silver medal in the hammer throw at the 1996 Atlanta Olympics?
A. Lance Deal.

Q. What wrestler who came from Missoula County High School won a bronze medal in the 1976 Montreal Olympics in wrestling?
A. Gene Davis.

Q. What Montanan has won more Olympic medals than any other Montanan, for shooting events at the 1964 Tokyo and 1972 Munich Olympics?

A. Lones Wigger Jr., two gold and one silver.

Q. What two-time world champ bull rider was also a model, movie stunt consultant, and CNN's Woman of the 80s?
A. Jonnie Jonckowski of Billings.

Q. What female rodeo star, famous for standing backwards on the rump of a galloping horse while twirling lassoes in each hand, starred in movies with Rudy Vallee?
A. Fanny Sperry Steele.

Q. In 1994 how old was Rachel Myllymaki of Arlee when she became the youngest rider ever to qualify for the National Finals Rodeo?
A. 11, placing ninth in barrel racing.

Q. What rodeo performer known as the "queen of the bronc riders" won four world saddle bronc championships and was the first inductee into the Cowgirl Hall of Fame?
A. Alice Greenough Orr of Red Lodge.

Q. How many members of the Greenough family of Red Lodge have been inducted into the Cowboy Hall of Fame in Oklahoma City?
A. Three: Turk Greenough, Margie Greenough Hensen, and Alice Greenough Orr, all inducted in 1983.

Q. Sheila Kirkpatrick of Twin Bridges was inducted into the National Cowboy Hall of Fame for her proficiency in what skill?
A. Making cowboy hats at her "Mad Hatter" studio. She's even made hats for Cheryl Ladd and Hank Williams, Jr.

Q. In the 1990s what Great Falls native racked up 36 victories in 40 professional boxing matches, including 32 knockouts?
A. Todd Foster.

Q. What member of the Salish Kootenai Nation of Montana became the first ever cruiserweight champion of the world?
A. Marvin Camel in 1980.

Q. What well-known prizefighter fought Tommy Gibbons in a heavyweight championship in Shelby on July 4, 1923, attracting a crowd estimated at around 20,000 in a town with a population of 1,000?
A. Jack Dempsey, who won, not by knockout, but by referee's decision. The event, fraught with fraud, nearly bankrupted Shelby.

Q. What Manhattan cowboy won saddle bronc championships at the National Rodeo Finals in 1993, 1994, 1995, 1997, and 1998?
A. Dan Mortensen.

Q. At the Fort Shaw Indian Boarding School in 1904, a team of women became world champions in what sport?
A. Basketball.

Q. What is the most commonly hunted game bird?
A. Ring-necked pheasants, with some 150,000 taken each year.

Q. In what year were ring-necked pheasants first introduced into Montana?
A. 1905.

Q. When was the first ring-necked pheasant hunting season?
A. 1928.

Q. The first wild turkeys were transplanted into the state in what year?
A. 1955, when 18 were released.

Q. When was the first turkey hunting season?
A. 1957.

Q. After the law made it illegal in 1915 to hunt rapidly diminishing bighorn sheep, how many years was it before limited hunting was allowed again?
A. 38.

Q. How long was the hunting season closed for moose?
A. 50 years, 1895-1945.

Q. How many bow-hunting licenses were purchased in 2000?
A. 26,000.

Q. Great Falls has been home to how many national champion figure skaters?
A. Two: Scott Davis (1993, 1994) and John Misha Petkevich (1971), both of whom competed in the Olympics.

Q. What tournament is named after the captain of the 1968 U.S. Olympic hockey team, a Great Falls native who was killed in a car accident in 1967 before he was to report for training?
A. The Terry Casey Memorial Cup Hockey Tournament.

Q. Utah State forward Wayne Estes was averaging 33.7 points in the 1964-65 season when he stopped to help a car accident victim and was electrocuted by a live wire. What town was he from?
A. Anaconda.

Q. What Butte native won the 5,000-meter World Cup speed-skating championship in 1986?
A. David Silk.

Q. Where was the original Marlboro man discovered?
A. At a rodeo in Augusta in the early 1960s.

Q. What did the original Marlboro man die of in 1995?
A. David McLean died of lung cancer and emphysema.

Q. What happened to sales of Marlboro cigarettes after the introduction of the first "Marlboro Men"?
A. Within eight months of the first Marlboro Man ad campaign, sales increased 5,000 percent.

Q. What was unusual about the 11 members of the Golden Bobcats basketball team of Montana State College in 1940?
A. All were killed in World War II.

Q. How many field goals did Forest Peters drop kick for Montana State College in a single game in 1924?
A. 17.

Q. The combined total distance of the passes completed at University of Montana by Dave Dickenson would be enough to clear what mountain?
A. Mount Everest, with room to spare. He passed for 11,080 yards.

Q. The Montana State University Bobcats won the NCAA Division I-AA football championship in what year?
A. 1984, beating Louisiana Tech.

Q. The University of Montana Grizzlies won the NCAA Division I-AA football championship in what years?
A. 1995 and 2001.

Q. The rivalry between the MSU Bobcats and the University of Montana Grizzlies, one of the longest-running annual competitions west of the Mississippi, began in what year?
A. 1897.

Q. What winningest coach in University of Montana history with a 75-35 record was named Division I-AA coach of the year by *American Football Quarterly* in 1995?
A. Don Read, who retired in 1996.

Q. Carroll College's new football stadium was named after what alumnus, who funded scholarships for more than 60 students?
A. Warren Nelson, class of 1931.

Q. As of 2004, how many consecutive years have the Carroll College Fighting Saints won the NAIA Football National Championship?
A. Three years in a row.

Q. Where was Meriwether Lewis standing when he first discovered cutthroat trout?
A. Great Falls of the Missouri River.

Q. What Montana town on the Missouri River has been dubbed the "trout capital of the world"?
A. Craig, population 40, where the trout outnumber the residents 400 to one.

Q. How many fish are around Craig, a town with 34 miles of blue ribbon trout fishing accessed by 12 recreation sites?
A. 5,000 per river mile.

Q. What town boasts that it's the home of "660 people and 11 million trout"?
A. Ennis.

Q. *Sports Afield* magazine named what Montana town as "the best place to catch trout in the world"?
A. Twin Bridges.

Q. What painter once held the record for striped bass and was better known as a fisherman than as an artist?
A. Russell Chatham.

Q. What author once wrote, "In our family, there was no clear line between religion and fly-fishing"?
A. Norman Maclean in *A River Runs Through It*.

Q. When traveling in the backcountry, who has the right-of-way: backpackers, pack strings, or horseback riders?
A. Pack strings.

Q. The 19 million acres of national forest in Montana are about the size of what eastern seaboard state?
A. South Carolina.

Q. Which of the state's 10 national forests is the largest, with 2.3 million acres?
A. Flathead, which is about the size of Delaware and Rhode Island combined.

Q. Are there more miles of trails or roads in Yellowstone?
A. 1,000 miles of trail versus 466 miles of roads.

Q. What is the only state that has more trails in national forests than Montana?
A. California.

Q. Throughout the state there are how many miles of marked hiking trails?
A. 14,633.

Q. How many miles of interstate highways are there throughout the state?
A. 1,200.

Q. How many miles of groomed snowmobile trails are in the state?
A. 3,700.

Q. The world's first KOA (Kampgrounds of America) campground appeared outside what town that is now company headquarters?
A. Billings.

Q. What kind of unusual accommodation is available to rent at Flathead State Park?
A. A yurt, sleeping six and including a propane barbecue grill.

Q. How many licensed outfitters are there statewide?
A. 661.

Q. What Montana town was named by *Outside* magazine the number one dream town for outdoor recreation?
A. Missoula.

Q. What town is known as the "Christmas tree capital of the world"?
A. Eureka.

Q. Montana's 75 Christmas tree farms cover how many acres?
A. Just over 1,000, compared to more than 17,000 acres in Michigan.

Q. Where in the state would you find the only working antique steam engine on a functioning railroad?
A. Virginia City, where it carries tourists the mile and a half to Nevada City and back.

Q. Are there any states that have more pick-up trucks per capita than the 361 trucks for every 1,000 residents in Montana?
A. Yes: North and South Dakota.

Q. Are there more snowmobiles or boats registered in the state?
A. Boats, with about 50,000 compared to 22,440 snowmobiles.

Q. Which is the only state that has a higher per capita rate of private airplane ownership than Montana?
A. Alaska.

Q. How many states have a gas tax higher than Montana's 27 cents per gallon?
A. Five: Washington, Wisconsin, Rhode Island, Illinois, and New York (highest at 32.7 cents per gallon). Lowest is Georgia at 7.5 cents.

Q. What percentage of Montana's approximately 70,000 miles of roads are paved?
A. 25 percent.

Q. What is the motto of the Testicle Festival held in Clinton every summer?
A. "I had a BALL at the testicle festival!"

Q. How many people attended the first Testicle Festival in 1982?
A. About 300.

Q. How many attended in 2000?
A. About 15,000 nuts.

Q. How many pounds of bull testicles were served?
A. 4,500.

Q. After agriculture, what is Montana's largest industry?
A. Tourism.

Q. Montana, with a population of under a million, receives how many tourists in a typical year?
A. 9.67 million, about 10 tourists for every resident.

Q. From what state do the greatest number of tourists come from?
A. California, followed by Washington and Texas.

Q. Which national park, Glacier or Yellowstone, has more visitors?
A. Yellowstone with more than three million per year. Glacier gets around two million.

Q. What percent of Americans have visited Yellowstone?
A. An estimated 30 percent.

Q. How many miles of rivers and streams are there statewide?
A. 21,100, of which 11,684 miles are polluted by metals, sediment, nutrients (including manure and agricultural runoff), and temperature.

Q. How many miles of rivers are federally designated Wild and Scenic Rivers?
A. 368.

Q. How many miles of rivers are officially classified as Blue Ribbon Streams because of their productivity, accessibility, and aesthetics?
A. 541 miles.

Q. Sections of what rivers receive the heaviest fishing pressure?
A. Missouri, Bighorn, and Bitterroot.

Q. What lakes receive the heaviest fishing pressure?
A. Canyon Ferry Reservoir, Fort Peck Reservoir, and Holter Reservoir.

Q. How many lakes are there in the state?
A. About 1,900, covering some 400,000 acres.

Q. How big is Mount Helena City Park, the second largest city park in the nation?
A. 880 acres, compared to Golden Gate Park in San Francisco with 1,017 acres and third-place Central Park in New York City with 843 acres.

Q. Beaver Creek County Park near Havre, the largest county park in the nation, has how many acres?
A. 10,000.

Q. Who is Butte's most famous son, who won the Class A Rocky Mountain Ski Association men's ski jumping championship in 1957?
A. Robert Knievel, later known as Evel.

Q. What Montanan was featured on *Wild World of Sports* in 1975, drawing the greatest viewing audience the show ever had?
A. Evel Knievel, jumping 14 Greyhound buses on his motorcycle.

Q. How many days did Evel Knievel spend in a coma after jumping 151 feet across the fountains of Caesar's Palace in Las Vegas in 1968?
A. 30 days, and he also suffered pelvic and hip fractures.

Q. When Evel Knievel asked his hometown of Butte to name a street after him, why did they refuse?
A. Because of his spotty reputation.

Q. What business is listed in the *Guinness Book of World Records* for turning standing wheat in a field into 13 loaves of bread in eight minutes, thirteen seconds?
A. Wheat Montana Farms and Bakery near Three Forks where they "sow it, grow it, and dough it."

Q. Who was the most well known person to receive a slice of the record-setting loaf?
A. A loaf was sent to President Bill Clinton.

Q. Each February the Winter Carnival in Whitefish holds a sculpture contest in what artistic medium?
A. Ice.

Q. What sporting events are highlighted at Missoula's Frost Fever Festival every February?
A. Snow football, snow softball, and snow volleyball.

Q. What event is held every New Year's Day at Wood's Bay on Flathead Lake near Big Fork?
A. The Polar Bear Plunge where hardy souls jump into the freezing lake.

Q. What do you call the Scandinavian sport in which a horse and rider pull a skier through an obstacle course?
A. Ski joring, the national finals of which are held at Red Lodge each March.

Q. Where can you enjoy an annual ski festival on the Fourth of July?
A. In Wibaux, where the area's large Polish population (having names that end in -*ski*) celebrate their heritage. Events include a greased "pole" climb.

Q. What do you call the rodeo event involving horses running at full gallop while dragging a clown balancing on a board?
A. North Dakota surfing.

Q. How is Christmas celebrated at Lewis and Clark Caverns State Park?
A. With a candlelight tour of the cave.

Q. What town hosts an annual Floating Flotilla boat parade every July, with decorated boats floated down the Beaverhead River?
A. Twin Bridges.

Q. What city sponsors the annual Cardboard Cup Regatta, where all boats entering the race must be made of cardboard, paint, duct tape, and nothing more?
A. Helena, at Spring Meadow Lake.

Q. What ski area hosts the Cardboard Cup Classic each winter, during which cardboard contraptions hit the slopes and are awarded prizes for the most creative?
A. Red Lodge Mountain.

Q. What sports team once stayed overnight in Wolf Creek after being refused rooms in both Helena and Great Falls because team members were black?
A. Harlem Globetrotters.

Q. In what city would you find the High Altitude Sports Center, the highest sports center in the world at 5,528 feet in elevation?
A. Butte.

Q. Where does the U.S. speed skating team train?
A. The High Altitude Sports Center in Butte.

Q. Former Governor Judy Martz was a member of the 1965 Winter Olympic Team competing for the United States in what sport?
A. Speed skating, finishing 15th, the best finish by a U.S. woman up to that time.

Q. What golfer designed and directed the construction of a $1 million golf course built on top of a Superfund site in Anaconda?
A. Jack Nicklaus, working over the contaminated mine tailings from the abandoned Anaconda Smelter. The black sand traps are made from mining slag.

Q. What golf tournament held every summer in Ringling (population forty) is sponsored by JT's Bar and Supper Club, the only business in town?
A. The PGA (Pasture Golf Association).

Q. What lady golfer from Kalispell has earned more than $1 million on LPGA tour?
A. Alice Ritzman, earning the second most by a player who has never won a tournament.

Q. What high school set a record by winning a WUSA wrestling championship every year between 1980 and 1992?
A. Butte High School.

Q. Between 1974 and 1984, what high school boy's cross-country running team won 11 state championships?
A. Browning High School on the Blackfeet Indian Reservation.

Q. Gene Davis of Missoula County High School won the state wrestling championship how many times?
A. Four, and four national freestyle championships.

Q. What well-known dog musher from Lincoln started calling himself the "Unamusher" after the Unabomber was arrested in Lincoln?
A. Doug Swingley.

Q. The only winner who doesn't live in Alaska, what Montana dog sled musher has won the 1,100-mile Iditarod in Alaska four different times?
A. Doug Swingley, the oldest champion at 45.

Q. How many times has musher Terry Adkins of Sand Coulee run the Iditarod?
A. 21, more than any other Montanan. His highest finish was 8th.

Q. Copper king Marcus Daly was most interested in what sport?
A. Racing horses, which he raised on his 22,000-acre ranch.

Q. How many Kentucky Derby winners came from the blood-lines of Marcus Daly's horses?
A. Five: Regret, Paul Jones, Zev, Flying Ebony, and Assault.

Q. What animal was memorialized on the floor of the Montana Hotel in Anaconda with a portrait made of inlaid parquet?
A. Marcus Daly's famous racehorse Tammany.

Q. The horse named Spokane, winner of the 1889 Kentucky Derby at six-to-one odds, came from a ranch near what town?
A. Twin Bridges.

Q. What golf great owns a hunting lodge near Noxon?
A. Jack Nicklaus.

Q. What two animals tie for first place in having the most Montana high school teams named after them?
A. Panther and Bulldog both claim nine high schools.

Q. High school sports teams in Belfry have what name?
A. The Bats.

Q. At what high school are the teams named the Copperheads?
A. The smelting town of Anaconda.

Q. At what high school are the teams named the Wardens?
A. Deer Lodge, home of the state prison.

Q. The Refiners are what high school's teams?
A. Sunburst, where oil was discovered in 1923.

Q. What high school won nationwide attention on *Late Night with David Letterman* for having the strangest mascot?
A. The Chinook High School Sugar Beeters.

Q. At Big Mountain near Whitefish each winter, what unusual ski competition takes place?
A. A furniture race, where skis are attached to any snow-worthy item of furniture and ridden down the mountain.

Q. What unusual ski competition is held at Showdown ski area near Neihart each winter?
A. Mannequin jumping, where decorated mannequins are attached to skis and sent down the mannequin ski jump.

Q. What town sponsors the Spam Cup cross-country ski race with a can of the much-maligned meat awarded the winner?
A. West Yellowstone.

Q. What events are included in the Double Pole, Pad, and Pedal Marathon at Bridger Bowl each April?
A. Downhill skiing, cross-country skiing, running, and bicycling.

Q. If you were participating in the Pinhead Classic Costume Race at Bridger Bowl, what kind of skiing would you be doing?
A. Telemark skiing, in which you must dress according to the theme, such as Space Odyssey in 2001, or Medieval Knievel.

Q. What was the only U.S. ski resort to host a telemark ski competition in 2000?
A. Big Mountain.

Q. Where was the telemark skiing originally developed?
A. Telemark, Norway.

Q. Jerry Kramer, an offensive guard who led the Green Bay Packers in scoring and was fourth in the league with 91 points in 1963, was born in what town?
A. Jordan.

Q. How many school records did Great Falls native Dave Dickenson break when he quarterbacked for University of Montana?
A. 13.

Q. What quarterback was awarded the 1995 Walter Payton Award for being the best player of Division I-AA?
A. Dave Dickenson, playing for the University of Montana Grizzlies.

Q. Who took over coaching of the Lady Griz in 1978 and not only turned them into a winning team but also boosted attendance at games from 200 to more than 5,000?
A. Robin Selvig.

Q. What University of Montana coach reached 600 career wins faster than all but five coaches in NCAA Division I history?
A. Robin Selvig, who reached the 600 milestone in only 772 games.

Q. Shannon Cate-Schweyen of Billings, all-time leading scorer, male or female, in Montana basketball history, scored how many points during her four seasons with the Lady Griz?
A. 2,172. She is now their assistant coach under Robin Selvig.

Q. Missoula-born Thomas Sven Moe became the first American Olympic athlete to win two medals in what?
A. Alpine skiing, in 1994 at the Olympics in Lillehammer, Norway.

Q. What controversial sport did Fish, Wildlife and Parks begin lobbying to ban in 2001?
A. Water skipping, in which a snowmobile travels at full throttle across open water trying to reach the opposite shore before sinking. Snowmobiles don't float.

Q. What sport would you be playing if you and four other team members were mounted on horses using long mallets to whack a bouncy rubber playground ball toward a goal while five opponents did the same?
A. Cowboy polo.

Q. What is the only ski area that rents ski bikes, contraptions that use skis instead of wheels on the slopes?
A. Snowbowl, near Missoula.

Q. What town hosts the annual Barstool Races each February, where barstools must be mounted on skis to enter?
A. Martin City.

Q. On what pass was North America's first luge run constructed, in 1965?
A. Lolo Pass near Lolo Hot Springs.

Q. U.S. Aerial Ski Team member Eric Bergoust, a Missoula native, took seventh place at the 1994 Olympics, a silver medal at the 1997 World Championships, and what at the 1998 Olympics in Japan?
A. A gold medal.

Q. What sportscaster from Big Timber owns a home near the Eagle Bend Golf Course in Big Fork?
A. Brent Musberger.

Q. How many professional football quarterbacks came from Great Falls?
A. Two: Dave Dickenson and Ryan Leaf, who both quarterbacked for the San Diego Chargers.

Q. What boxer from Great Falls won the National Golden Gloves championship and the National Olympic Festival championship in 1987?
A. Todd Foster.

Q. Approximately how many campgrounds are there in the state?
A. More than 600.

Q. How many dude and guest ranches are there in the state?
A. About 150.

Q. How many horses are there in Montana?
A. A state survey in 1999 showed that there are at least 130,000 horses in Montana.

Q. Dick Randall of Montana's first dude ranch, the OTO, nearly a century ago declared, "If, after you've spent a month on a Montana ranch, riding horseback everyday and living outdoors, you don't feel better, you don't need a doctor, you need ____?"
A. An undertaker.

Q. How many states have a higher percentage of residents who are considered to be physically active?
A. Only three: Colorado, Washington State, and New Mexico.

Q. How many McDonald's restaurants are in Manhattan, New York (population 1.5 million)?
A. 74, about three per square mile.

Q. How many McDonald's restaurants are in Montana?
A. 29, one for every 5,000 square miles.

Q. How many McDonald's restaurants are in Manhattan, Montana (population 1,400)?
A. None.

Sports & Leisure Crossword

Across

1. Annual ski festival held in July in what town
3. How many seconds does a bull rider have to stay on to qualify in a rodeo
5. What do 57% of Montanans own at least one of
6. Where is the only working steam engine in the state
8. Number of McDonalds in Manhattan, MT
11. Which Montana national park has more visitors
12. Only state with more trails in national forests
14. Anaconda's high school teams are named what
15. "Snowmobile capital of the world"
18. Jerry Kramer was born in this town
19. Most recently added to the state park system
20. Smallest state park
21. Ski area that rents ski bikes

Down

2. Most vertical feet of ski area in the nation is found where
3. Town of 660 people, 11 million trout
4. Largest state park
7. Where is annual Floating Flotilla boat parade held
9. Butte's most famous son
10. Most commonly hunted big game animal in Montana
13. Montana school recognized on David Letterman show
14. More than 600 exist in Montana
16. There are 361 of these for every 1,000 residents
17. First luge constructed here

Answers on Page 154

ENTERTAINMENT

Q. The building that houses the Myrna Loy Performing Arts Center in Helena formerly housed what?
A. Prisoners—it was the county jail.

Q. The Copper Village Museum and Arts Center in Anaconda is in the building that originally had what function?
A. Government, as it was City Hall.

Q. The seven percent state sales tax on accommodations, designed to raise money for promoting tourism, funds what office?
A. The Montana Film Office, designed to attract moviemakers to the state.

Q. How many movies were shot in Montana between 1897 and 2003?
A. 97.

Q. In the 1952 film *Montana Belle*, what buxom star played a bandit queen involved with the Dalton Gang?
A. Jane Russell.

Q. In the 1982 movie *The Legend of Walks Far Woman*, what bosomy leading lady starred as an outcast Blackfeet Indian in 1875 Montana?
A. Raquel Welch.

Q. What Montana paleontologist served as the model for Sam Neil's character of Dr. Grant in the *Jurassic Park* movies?
A. Jack Horner.

Q. What 1991 movie depicting the life and times of General George Custer was filmed very near the actual site of Custer's Last Stand?
A. *Son of the Morning Star*.

Q. What famous newscaster, born in Cardwell, was the driving force behind the construction of the Big Sky ski resort town, but died three days before the grand opening ceremonies?
A. Chet Huntley.

Q. What 1981 film starring John Belushi as a city slicker pretending to be a nature lover was filmed partially in Glacier Park?
A. *Continental Divide*.

Q. How many towns in the state have a full symphony orchestra?
A. Seven: Billings, Butte, Bozeman, Great Falls, Helena, Kalispell, and Missoula.

Q. What's the smallest town in Montana that has an orchestra?
A. Scobey, with a population of 1,000, features 40 players in the "Prairie Symphonette."

Q. What actor in the TV series *Dallas* was born on St. Patrick's Day in Montana, and was named accordingly?
A. Patrick Duffy.

Q. What Great Falls bar, noted for its mermaids, was listed in the April 2003 "Gentlemen's Quarterly" magazine as one of the top ten bars in the world?
A. The Sip -N- Dip, where mermaids frolic in a 22,000-gallon pool while patrons watch them through the glass walls.

Q. What actress, while filming the movie *Northfork,* tried on a mermaid costume and took a dip in the Sip -N- Dip pool, recreating a former movie role?
A. Daryl Hannah re-created her role from the 1984 film *Splash* when she took a dip at the Sip -N- Dip in 1997.

Q. A bridge over the Missouri River near Craig was the scene for the climatic shootout between FBI men and gangsters in what movie starring Sean Connery and Kevin Costner?
A. *The Untouchables*.

Q. Joan Melcher's book *Watering Hole* is about what subject?
A. Montana bars.

Q. In the town of Two Dot, population 76, what's the motto of the Two Dot Saloon?
A. "Easy to find, hard to leave!"

Q. What's the motto of the Roadkill Café in McLeod?
A. "From Your Grille to Ours!"

Q. What popular female artist of the 1970s made famous the song "Meet Me In Montana" in a duet with Dan Seals?
A. Marie Osmond.

Q. While hunting near Missoula in 1975, what country singer fell 442 feet down a mountainside and had to spend two years in recovery?
A. Hank Williams, Jr., who suffered a skull fracture and facial injuries.

Q. Written and produced by Montanans, what 1979 movie based on the frontier diaries of Elinore Randall Stewart was filmed near Harlowton?
A. *Heartland,* which in real life took place in Wyoming.

Q. How many silver dollars are reputed to cover the walls and ceilings of the Silver Dollar Bar in DeBorgia?
A. Nearly 40,000.

Q. What well-known country singer once lived in Helena and Great Falls, where he played semi-professional baseball?
A. Charlie Pride.

Q. What country star sang a song called "Big City" in which he wanted the big city to "turn me loose, set me free somewhere in the middle of Montana"?
A. Merle Haggard.

Q. How many people did Norma Ashby interview during her 26-year career as host of the daily TV show called "Today in Montana"?
A. About 26,000.

Q. Norma Ashby spearheaded the drive to designate what state animal?
A. An avid fisherman, she pushed for adoption of a state fish. Blackspotted cutthroat trout was chosen.

Q. The opening scenes in the movie *The Shining* starring Jack Nicholson were filmed on what Montana highway?
A. Going-to-the-Sun Road in Glacier National Park.

Q. Well known for her scat singing and for her trombone playing, what native Montana jazz musician is a great-niece of Myrna Loy?
A. M.J. Williams.

Q. What Helena jazz musician makes a habit of staging his concerts in canyons, at campgrounds, and on mountaintops?
A. Wilbur Rehmann.

Q. Before entertaining his audience, what Montana folk singer is known for leading them on a wagon ride and feeding them dinner in a tipi?
A. Bruce Anfinson.

Q. What theater group tours schools around the world each year, encouraging some 50,000 kids to get up onstage and perform?
A. Missoula Children's Theater.

Q. What Western author and artist played a bit part in the 1946 Hollywood adaptation of his book *Smokey*?
A. Will James, a big turn-around for a man who was once imprisoned for cattle rustling.

Q. In what town can you tour an entire underground business district built after fire swept through town in 1904, destroying the aboveground business district?
A. Havre.

Q. Gene Autry crooned his way down the road while trailing pelt smugglers in what 1939 film?
A. *Blue Montana Skies.*

Q. Inspired by the town of Ringling, what pop singer wrote the lines, "Ringling, Ringling, slipping away / Only forty people living there today"?
A. Jimmy Buffett, in his song "Ringling, Ringling."

Q. Jimmy Buffett wrote the score for what 1975 movie, based on a novel by Montana resident Tom McGuane, about a couple of goofy cattle rustlers out for a good time?
A. *Rancho Deluxe.*

Q. In what song does Jimmy Buffett invite the listener to "sing a song, play some pong, shoot a little pool"?
A. "Livingston Saturday Night." Buffet owns property near Livingston.

Q. What 2002 film, set and filmed in Montana, starred Ryan Gosling playing quarterback on a six-man football team?
A. *The Slaughter Rule.* The Slaughter Rule stops a game whenever one team has a huge, insurmountable lead over the other team.

Q. What place in Ireland had a rollicking quick-step song named after it, which became the marching song of Custer's Seventh Cavalry and is now the name of a Montana town?
A. Garryowen, which is Irish for "garden of Owen."

Q. In what 1952 Western did Kirk Douglas star as a frontiersman who must deliver a Blackfeet princess to her father?
A. *The Big Sky,* loosely based on the novel by A. B. Guthrie, Jr.

Q. In what movie did Dustin Hoffman star as Jack Crabb, the only white survivor of the battle of the Little Big Horn?
A. *Little Big Man.*

Q. The folks in Saco set a world record in 1999 by cooking what 6,000-pound item, taking the title from Seymour, Wisconsin?
A. A hamburger— Seymour regained the title with an 8,266-pound burger the next year.

Q. How many cows went into Saco's 6,000-pound burger?
A. 17. Leftovers the next day included biscuits and gravy for breakfast and sloppy joes for dinner.

Q. What film starring Brad Pitt and Anthony Hopkins involved three brothers fighting over a single woman on a Montana ranch?
A. *Legends of the Fall,* an adaptation of the novel by part-time Montana resident and author Jim Harrison.

Q. For many years before his election, Senator Conrad Burns followed what career?
A. Radio announcing and television broadcasting, especially of agricultural reports. He was also an auctioneer.

Q. Where does Jim Nabors, the star of *Gomer Pyle* and costar *of The Andy Griffith Show* live?
A. Whitefish.

Q. Actor Frank James Cooper, Helena native, changed his name to what because there was already an actor named Frank Cooper?
A. Gary Cooper, because his agent was from Gary, Indiana.

Q. How many films did Gary Cooper make in his 36-year career?
A. Nearly 100, winning two Oscars for best actor (*High Noon* and *Sergeant York*) and a career achievement Academy Award.

Q. What country singer/songwriter who lived in the Bitterroot wrote the song "The Pusher" performed by Steppenwolf and used in the film *Easy Rider*?
A. Hoyt Axton.

Q. Joseph E. Howard, who wrote the music for "I Wonder Who's Kissing Her Now" and the Montana state song, "Montana," also wrote what popular ragtime tune of 1899?
A. "Hello, Ma Baby!" ("Hello, ma honey, hello, ma ragtime gal...")

Q. Who wrote the lyrics for the state song?
A. Charles Cohen, city editor of the *Butte Miner.*

Q. What state song sounds uncannily like a high school football cheer?
A. Montana. "Gimme an M...Gimme an O...Gimme an N...What's that spell? Montana!"

Q. Jon Voight, Barbara Hershey, Rich Schroder, and Louis Gossett Jr. starred in what Larry McMurtry sequel in which a herd of wild mustangs was driven 2,500 miles from Texas to Montana?
A. *Return to Lonesome Dove*.

Q. How much did it cost to build a ranch house near Billings on the set of *Return to Lonesome Dove* and to furnish it with period antiques?
A. $500,000.

Q. What happened to the ranch house and the entire collection of authentic antiques?
A. The house and all of its one-of-a-kind antiques were torched for a fiery climactic scene.

Q. What Montana town gave birth to the game of keno when a cigar store manager adapted it from a Chinese gambling game and then took it to Las Vegas?
A. Butte.

Q. What actor impersonates Charlie Russell, telling stories, jokes, and yarns from the famous Montana painter's point of view?
A. Raphael Cristy.

Q. What nickname did Big Sky singer and songwriter Jim Stoltz receive after spending years hiking over 25,000 miles around the world, carrying his guitar?
A. Walkin' Jim.

Q. What dinner train takes riders on the old Milwaukee Railroad line through scenic landscapes that inspired painter Charlie Russell?
A. The "Charlie Russell Chew-Choo" in Lewistown.

Q. The 1954 film *Cattle Queen of Montana,* filmed in Glacier National Park and the Flathead valley, starred Barbara Stanwyck acting with what leading man?
A. Ronald Reagan.

40th President Ronald Reagan

Q. What town hosts the annual Montana Cowboy Poetry gathering every August?
A. Lewistown.

Q. What actor, born in Helena and raised in White Sulphur Springs, was a regular on *The A Team* and also appeared in *Hawaii Five-O* and *Battle Star Galactica*?
A. Dirk Benedict.

Q. What stand-up comedian and *Saturday Night Live* cast member was born in Missoula?
A. Dana Carvey.

Q. During his day, what Helena-born actor was the highest paid actor in America?
A. Gary Cooper, who demanded half a million dollars per film in the 1940s and once starred in 11 movies made in an 18-month period.

Q. What Montana author wrote the screenplay for Jack Schaefer's *Shane*?
A. A. B. Guthrie, Jr.

Q. What actor starred in *Shane* and owns property near Ennis?
A. Ben Johnson.

Q. What paleontologist, born in Shelby, served as advisor for the *Jurassic Park* series?
A. Jack Horner.

Q. How old was paleontologist Jack Horner when he found his first dinosaur bone?
A. Jack, whose father owned a sand and gravel business, found his first dinosaur bone at age seven.

Q. What singer, actress, and comedienne did so much to entertain troops during World War II and the Vietnam War that upon her death in 1994 she was honored by being buried in the military cemetery at Fort Bragg, North Carolina?
A. Martha Raye, born in Butte.

Q. The 1993 film *Beethoven's 2nd*, sequel to the 1992 film *Beethoven*, starred a Saint Bernard and was filmed in part in what national park?
A. Glacier.

Q. How many Saint Bernard puppies were involved in making the movie?
A. 44. They kept growing up over the course of the filming and had to be replaced by younger puppies.

Q. What actress, born in 1980, was a cast member playing Jen on *Dawson's Creek* as well as appearing in many films?
A. Michelle Williams, born in Kalispell.

Q. What Emmy and Tony Award-winning choreographer and director of such movies as *Joy Luck Club* and *Return of the Jedi* was born in Missoula?
A. Michael Smuin, now director of Smuin Ballet of San Francisco.

Q. What 1989 Steven Spielberg movie filmed in Montana, starring Holly Hunter and Richard Dreyfuss, was Audrey Hepburn's final film?
A. *Always*, about forest firefighters.

Q. What actress, dubbed "queen of the movies" in a 1936 nationwide poll, was born in the tiny town of Radersburg, south of Helena?
A. Myrna Loy, who played Nora Charles alongside William Powell in the *Thin Man* series.

Q. Scenic shots of Glacier National Park figure prominently in what 1998 film starring Robin Williams who plays a dead man trying to help his living wife?
A. *What Dreams May Come*.

Q. When right-handed Gary Cooper portrayed left-handed Lou Gehrig in *The Pride of the Yankees,* how was the problem overcome?
A. Cooper played right-handed wearing a baseball uniform with the insignia sewn on backwards and then the film was flipped over.

Q. What martial arts movie star with a ponytail owns property near Ennis?
A. Steven Seagal.

Q. The tragic story of the flight of the Cheyenne from Oklahoma to Montana in 1878 inspired John Ford to make what pro-Indian movie in 1964?
A. *Cheyenne Autumn*—he wanted to make amends for casting Indians as villains in so many of his westerns.

Q. Held each August, what is the largest Native American gathering in the country?
A. The Crow Fair, on the Little Bighorn River near the site of Custer's Last Stand, attracting about 45,000 spectators and participants.

Q. Based on a true story of the sheep ranching country of 1880s Montana, what 1992 film starred Suzy Amis disguised as a man?
A. *The Ballad of Little Joe.*

Q. Born in Puerto Rico, what operatic baritone moved to Bozeman, where he created the Intermountain Opera Association?
A. Pablo Elvira, who died in 2000.

Q. Walter Van Tilburg Clark, who later taught English at the University of Montana, explored the subject of lynchings, mob justice, and vigilantes in what book, which was made into a movie in 1943?
A. *The Ox-Bow Incident.*

Q. Dorothy Johnson of Whitefish wrote what book that was made into a movie in 1962, starring John Wayne and James Stewart and directed by John Ford?
A. *The Man Who Shot Liberty Valance.*

Q. Photoplayers, huge organs used in movie theaters during the silent film era to provide music and sound effects, are rare today, but where in Montana can you find one?
A. Virginia City Opera House—only four are known to exist today.

Q. Where was the 16-foot-wide Cremona Photoplayer accidentally located in 1950?
A. In Deer Lodge, found during remodeling behind a wall in a drugstore constructed when a theater was turned into retail space.

Q. The plot of what Clint Eastwood/Jeff Bridges 1974 movie revolved around the robbery of a Montana government vault?
A. *Thunderbolt and Lightfoot.*

Q. Where in the state would you find the oldest continuously operated summer theater in the Northwest, established in 1949?
A. Virginia City, where the Virginia City Players perform in the Opera House.

Q. The 1996 film *Amanda* starred Kieran Culkin as a boy learning to trust horses on a ranch near what Montana town?
A. Red Lodge.

Q. What made-in-Montana movie involved a young boy who pledged to give up Little League baseball until nuclear weapons have been eliminated?
A. *Amazing Grace and Chuck.*

Q. What celebrity who first saw Montana during the filming of Tom McGuane's *Rancho Deluxe* later moved to the state?
A. Peter Fonda.

Q. What actor, who owns a home in the state, met his wife, Sue, while starring in the film *Rancho Deluxe* on location in Montana?
A. Jeff Bridges.

Q. What 1989 comedy, starring Lou Diamond Phillips and Fred Gwynne, was filmed in Hamilton and the Bitterroot Valley?
A. *Disorganized Crime.*

Q. What 1979 movie filmed in Montana, a $40 million-dollar flop, was one of the biggest money-losers of all time?
A. *Heaven's Gate.*

Q. What barefoot movie actor once rocked Chico Hot Springs with an impromptu two-hour rock-n-roll concert accompanied by his back-up band, the Sharks?
A. Dennis Quaid, who lived nearby.

Q. What actress, once voted one of the "fifty most beautiful people in the world" by *People* magazine, maintains a home in the Paradise Valley named Camp Warren Oates after the actor who sold it to her?
A. Meg Ryan.

Q. What fashion designer maintains a home near Lincoln?
A. Liz Claiborne.

Q. At the Museum of the Plains Indian in Browning, what actor narrates the multimedia presentation about the evolution of Native American cultures?
A. Vincent Price.

Q. On what river was part of *The River Wild* starring Meryl Streep and Kevin Bacon filmed?
A. The Kootenai.

Q. Filmed in Montana and directed by Robert Redford, what movie involved a rancher who had a mysterious healing connection with horses?
A. *The Horse Whisperer.*

Q. The film *Far and Away*, directed by Ron Howard, involving Irish immigrants in the Oklahoma land rush, was shot near what city?
A. Billings.

Q. What national network newscaster has homes in New York and Montana?
A. Tom Brokaw.

Q. The 1995 film *Broken Arrow* starring John Travolta and Christian Slater, filmed near Lewistown, dealt with what kind of stolen weapons?
A. Nuclear warheads.

Q. Bob Fletcher, who wrote the text for more than 100 Montana highway historical markers, wrote a poem that became the lyrics for what big hit by Cole Porter?
A. "Don't Fence Me In."

Q. When Myrna Loy, then Myrna Williams, moved from her birthplace of Radersburg to Helena, she lived down the block from what future movie actor?
A. Gary Cooper, who was four years older than she was.

Q. How many films did Myrna Loy make during a career that spanned seven decades?
A. More than 117.

Q. In what town would you find only one business, a tavern called the Polar Bar?
A. Polaris.

Q. Martha Jane Cannary, who moved to Virginia City in 1865 with her family as a teen, became a famous sharpshooter using what stage name?
A. Calamity Jane.

Q. In the 1989 film *Cold Feet*, filmed near Livingston and starring Jeff Bridges and Keith Carradine, where were the smuggled emeralds hidden?
A. Inside a horse.

Q. What story was written by Montanan Dorothy Johnson and made into a movie starring Montanan Gary Cooper?
A. *The Hanging Tree.*

Q. What famous heartthrob, star of such movies as *Braveheart* and the *Lethal Weapon* series, owns a working cattle ranch in Montana?
A. Mel Gibson.

Q. What lost but highly acclaimed Montana classic was found and published in 2003 by Bedrock Editions and Riverbend Publishing of Helena?
A. *On Sarpy Creek* by Ira Nelson, originally published in 1938, and the only book he ever wrote.

Q. Based on the 1949 tragedy of Mann Gulch where thirteen firefighters died, what 1952 movie starred Richard Widmark?
A. *Red Skies Over Montana.*

Q. Shirley Temple made what movie that featured shots of Glacier National Park, with Blackfeet filling in as extras?
A. *Susannah of the Mounties.*

Q. Known as the "fishing poet" of Montana State University, what professor has written poems about neoprene waders, songs about hot dogs, and has a CD called *Live from Nowhere?*
A. Greg Keeler, a "fool" professor at MSU.

Q. What group of musical ranchers is known for their lampooning and lambasting, as well as their musical skill?
A. The Ringling Five.

Q. In the 1993 film *Josh and S.A.M.*, filmed largely in Montana, what is a S.A.M.?
A. Strategically Altered Mutant.

Q. Why was Montana chosen as a main location for filming film *Josh and S.A.M.?*
A. Producers wanted a single state that could look like seven different states.

Q. What 1998 comedy partially filmed in Montana starred Chris Farley and Matthew Perry playing explorers who were trying to beat Lewis and Clark to the Pacific?
A. *Almost Heroes.*

Q. What degree did Carroll O'Conner, Archie Bunker on *All in the Family*, earn from University of Montana in 1956?
A. Master of Fine Arts.

Q. In the movie *Iron Will*, based on a true story and filmed in part in the Madison Range, Mackenzie Astin stars as Will Stoneman, who must win what kind of a race to save the family farm?
A. Sled dog.

Q. What city hosts the International Wildlife Film Festival, the largest, longest-running festival of its kind in the world?
A. Missoula, attended by about 10,000 people.

Q. Montana author Dan Cushman wrote the book *Stay Away, Joe* which was made into a film starring what movie star?
A. Elvis Presley.

Q. Robert Corbett, founder of the National Affordable Housing Network, lives in what sort of house in Butte?
A. A solar-heated home made from a converted 50-foot-tall, 1,000-ton zinc ore storage bin.

Q. How did Robert Corbett, known artistically as OXO, turn his 1970 Oldsmobile into the "shiniest car on earth"?
A. By covering it bumper to bumper with 694 mirror pieces.

Q. What designation is on Corbett's vanity license plate?
A. SHINY.

Q. How old was John "The Yank" Harrington of Butte in 1999 when he released his first CD of Irish accordion tunes called *A Celtic Century?*
A. 96. He died in 2004.

Q. What singer and songwriter is known for her seminars that empower women through music?
A. Judy Fjell of Big Timber.

Q. What Montana singer and songwriter has worked on ads for Levi 501 jeans, Coors beer, and Amtrak?
A. Rob Quist.

Q. What Bozeman dancer worked as choreographer on the set of the movie *The Horse Whisperer?*
A. Katherine Kramer.

Q. The Irish band Dublin Gulch is named after what?
A. A historic Irish neighborhood in Butte.

Q. When Frank Zappa wrote a song called "Montana" about "moving to Montana soon," what was he going to do once he got to Montana?
A. Become a dental floss tycoon.

Q. The cultural roundup held in Cut Bank each April is devoted to what?
A. Storytelling, at the Montana Storytelling Roundup.

Q. The Montana Logging and Ballet Company mounts what kind of productions?
A. Music, comedy, and satire.

Q. In the film *Me and Will*, two motorcycle mamas trek on their bikes to Montana in search of what?
A. Peter Fonda's bike in *Easy Rider* located in a junkyard.

Q. What best-selling Montana historian and novelist wrote the screenplay for *Band of Brothers* and served as a consultant for the Steven Speilberg movie *Saving Private Ryan*?
A. Stephen Ambrose.

Q. The 1991 autobiography *Confessions of a Kamikaze Cowboy* was written by what Montana-born actor?
A. Dirk Benedict.

Q. Before its restoration, the Alberta Bair Theater in Billings, the last art deco style theater built by 20ᵗʰ Century Fox, was almost demolished to make room for what?
A. A parking garage or a three-screen movieplex.

Q. Norman Maclean wrote about what river in his book *A River Runs Through It*?
A. The Blackfoot.

Q. Where was the movie *A River Runs Through It* filmed?
A. In Bozeman, Livingston, and Seeley Lake because the Blackfoot River was too difficult to set up scenes.

Q. What Montana musician performed the solo piano soundtrack for *The Velveteen Rabbit* and *This Is America, Charlie Brown* and the guitar soundtrack for *Sadako and the Thousand Paper Cranes*?
A. George Winston.

Q. Where was the film *Everything That Rises*, starring Dennis Quaid as a Montana rancher, filmed?
A. In the Paradise Valley, near Quaid's property.

Q. The part of a truck that prevents gravel from hitting the windshield of the vehicles behind is the name of what popular Montana dance band?
A. The Big Sky Mudflaps.

Q. The 1940s jazz pianist Jean Wrobel chose what surname, based on her hometown, as her stage name, while retaining her real first name?
A. Hamilton.

Q. Eden Atwood, jazz singer, pianist, and composer, is the granddaughter of what noted Montana author?
A. A. B. Guthrie, Jr.

Q. What city hosts the International Choral Festival every third year, hosting choirs from 29 different countries in recent years?
A. Missoula.

Q. Jazz pianist Don Pullen and his African-Brazilian Connection collaborated with the Chief Cliff Singers of what tribe to produce *Sacred Common Ground* in 1995, his final work before his death?
A. Confederated Salish and Kootenai Tribe of Elmo, Montana.

Q. What pop star, who owns property in the Bitterroot Valley, earned $150 for his first concert, which was given in Europe?
A. Huey Lewis.

Q. The book *Falling Angel* by Montana novelist William Hjortsberg was made into what 1987 movie about murder, mystery, and the occult?
A. *Angel Heart*.

Q. In the 1994 movie *Holy Matrimony* directed by Leonard Nimoy, where does the thief, played by Patricia Arquette, hide out until things settle down?
A. A Hutterite colony, supposedly in Alberta but actually shot near Great Falls.

Q. Hoyt Axton, who lived in the Bitterroot Valley, wrote what signature song that was a hit for Three Dog Night?
A. "Joy to the World" ("Jeremiah was a bullfrog...")

Q. What Missoula woman was not only executive producer of the prize-winning film *Heartland* but was also co-producer of Robert Redford's Academy Award-winning *A River Runs Through It*?
A. Annick Smith.

Q. When did Montana Shakespeare in the Parks begin the program of bringing classic plays to small communities that otherwise might not get a chance to experience Shakespeare?
A. 1973—it has given more than 1,500 performances since then.

Q. Jeff Bridges purchased the ranch that was used as the setting of a brothel in what made-in-Montana flop that he starred in?
A. *Heaven's Gate*.

Q. What pianist and composer performed in the MSU Chamber Music Festival for four years while he was attending high school?
A. Philip Aaberg.

Q. What classical guitarist with Montana roots teaches a summer master class at MSU and received an honorary doctorate of music from the university?
A. Christopher Parkening.

Q. Where would you find a manufacturing plant turning out Gibson Guitars?
A. Bozeman.

Q. In 1918 one of America's first feature-length color films, *Cupid Angling* with Mary Pickford and Douglas Fairbanks, was partially filmed in what national park?
A. Yellowstone.

Q. Operatic soprano Judith Blegan, who has performed at Carnegie Hall and with the Metropolitan Opera, grew up in what Montana town?
A. Missoula.

Q. What Greek/Montana songwriter, who goes by only a single name, has written a string of top ten hits including "Turn It On, Turn It Up, Turn Me Loose" and "Lord Have Mercy on the Working Man"?
A. Kostas.

Q. What singer/songwriter, named entertainer of the year three times by the Academy of Country Music and twice by the Country Music Association, owns property near Wisdom?
A. Hank Williams, Jr.

Q. *Men's Journal* was referring to what town in its 1998 review of "25 Great Places" with this description: " 'Hay/Seed' is a heading in the town paper's classifieds, not necessarily a description of the typical resident"?
A. Lewistown.

Q. The 1950 movie *Montana* starred what swashbuckling actor who crooned the tune, "I Reckon I'm Falling in Love" as a ploy to find out who murdered a sheepherder?
A. Errol Flynn.

Q. The 1992 made-for-TV movie *Montana* starring Gena Rowlands and Richard Crenna, was based on a story written by what author?
A. Larry McMurtry.

Q. In the 1998 film *Montana,* which involved double-crosses, kidnappings, and shootouts, why did the big city criminals speak wistfully of Montana?
A. Because it is an ideal place to go to when their criminal days are over.

Q. What brawny leading man, the star of horse operas, romantic comedies, and musicals, was born the youngest of fifteen children in 1916 in Brady and was raised on the family homestead there?
A. George Montgomery.

Q. Dinah Shore was married for two decades to what Montana native?
A. George Montgomery.

Q. Who played the title role in the 1971 movie *Evel Knievel* based on the life of this Butte native?
A. George Hamilton.

Q. Who played the title role in the 1977 drug-smuggling thriller *Viva Knievel?*
A. Evel Knievel.

Q. What town was home to the Dumas, America's longest-operating house of ill repute, which opened in 1890, closed in 1982, and later reopened as a museum dedicated to the lifestyle?
A. Butte.

Q. What rodeo queen from Red Lodge did trick riding in the 1937 film *The Californians* and did stunt work on the TV series *Little House on the Prairie?*
A. Alice Greenough Orr.

Q. Served at barbecues all around the state, what unusual kind of fondue does Lloyd Wolery specialize in?
A. Pitchfork fondue, where steaks are skewered on pitchforks and deep fat fried.

Q. What actor from Montana turned down the role of Rhett Butler in *Gone With the Wind?*
A. Gary Cooper.

Q. In what rock band does Big Sandy native Jeff Ament play bass, which in 1988 gave a concert of their new album *Yield* at the football stadium in Missoula, where they attracted 22,000 fans—one of the state's largest crowds?
A. Pearl Jam.

Q. What filmmaker born in Missoula directed such films as *Dune, Blue Velvet, Wild at Heart, Lost Highway,* and *Mulholland Drive?*
A. David Lynch.

Q. What made-in-Montana movie about fly-fishing used actors who had never before held a fly-fishing rod?
A. *A River Runs Through It*.

Q. In the film *Forrest Gump* when Tom Hanks ran through wheat fields in Montana and across a bridge in Glacier, who doubled for him during the filming?
A. His real-life brother Jim.

Q. In Ingomar (population 118) what is the answer to a bed and breakfast?
A. The Bunk and Biscuit, always full during hunting season.

Q. In 1989 what event drew 3,000 cattle, 3,500 horses, 3,000 riders, and 300 wagons to the town of Roundup?
A. The Great Montana Centennial Cattle Drive, celebrating the state's 100th birthday.

Q. When Native American songwriter Jack Gladstone released a CD entitled *Buffalo Café*, what did the title refer to?
A. The great grasslands that once fed huge bison herds.

Q. What is unique about the carousel in the Great Northern Town Center of Helena?
A. It features animals native to Montana, such as bison and bighorn sheep.

Q. What town celebrates the Chokecherry Festival each September, which includes a culinary contest, awards for best art made from its leaves and wood, and pit-spitting contests?
A. Lewistown.

Q. Park City sponsors what type of unusual races every August?
A. Lawnmower.

Q. Where could you participate in the annual Flapjack Race, where rules dictate that you must build a fire and cook an edible pancake, all while keeping your untied mule within 15 feet of you at all times?
A. Montana Mule Days in Drummond each June.

Q. The Philipsburg Opera House hosts what musical celebration each year?
A. The Rocky Mountain Accordion Celebration.

Q. How would you win a game of cow-pie bingo at Flint Creek Valley Days in Philipsburg?
A. A cow is put into a fenced field that has been marked with a bingo grid, and the winner is the one who correctly guesses which square the first cow pie will land in.

Q. Where can you go to bet on the pig races?
A. Bearcreek's 50 residents hold Pig Races each summer weekend as a fundraiser. Pigs are tended by local "sowboys."

Q. What town hosts the annual "Punkin' Chuckin' Contest" to see who can build a device to throw an eight-pound pumpkin the farthest without using motors or explosives?
A. Missoula, where the current record is nearly 4,000 feet. Proceeds support a local youth organization.

Q. What's the average estimated attendance at the St. Patrick's Day Parade in Butte each year?
A. About 30,000 in a town whose total population is about 34,000.

Q. What is Reed Point's answer to Pamplona's Running of the Bulls?
A. The annual Running of the Sheep, including the Sheep Roundup, the Sheep Beauty Contest, and skydiving (plastic) sheep.

Q. In the middle of July, where would you find, for one day each year, a beverage bar carved out of a snowbank?
A. The Beartooth Highway, where the Red Lodge Chamber of Commerce hosts the "Top of the World Bar."

Q. What annual Montana event has repeatedly been listed as one of the "top one hundred events in America" by *Destinations* magazine and has been filmed by A & E, CNN, and BBC?
A. The re-enactment of Custer's Last Stand.

Q. The Sunshine Station in what town will treat you to a beverage on the house any day the sun doesn't shine?
A. Philipsburg.

Q. What town hosts the Super Bull, a bull-riding competition each June?
A. Wolf Point.

Q. Benny Goodman Park in Anaconda was named after a man with what connection to the town?
A. Former mayor, not the clarinetist.

Q. David Lynch, born in Missoula, co-wrote and directed what popular television series that debuted in 1989 and lasted two seasons, attracting a cult-like following?
A. *Twin Peaks.*

Q. Who abandoned the family ranch north of Helena to become an actor because "getting up at 5:00 in the morning in the dead of winter to feed 450 cows at 40 below ain't romantic"?
A. Gary Cooper.

Q. What Montanan wrote the screenplay for *The Kentuckian* in 1955?
A. A. B. Guthrie.

Q. John Dillinger was gunned down outside the Biograph Theatre in Chicago after seeing *Manhattan Melodrama* starring what Montana actress whom he adored?
A. Myrna Loy.

Q. Michael Keaton, star of *Mr. Mom* and *Batman*, owns a ranch near what town?
A. McLeod.

Q. In the summer of 2000, what unusual honor was bestowed upon Willie Nelson when he gave a concert in Red Lodge?
A. A forest fire that started on the day he was there was named the Willie Fire after him. It burned about 1,500 acres.

Q. In what town can you see the water of Spring Creek running under the Montana Tavern through a hole in the floor?
A. Lewistown.

Q. Smithsonian Institution ranked the art deco Washoe Theater in what town as the fifth best in the nation for its architecture?
A. Anaconda.

Q. The opening scene of the 1981 film *Fast Walking* starring James Woods as a prison guard who helped a militant African American prisoner escape, was filmed at what location?
A. The Montana State Prison in Deer Lodge.

Q. In the movie *Triumphs of a Man Called Horse* which was filmed in Montana, what actor played an English inductee to the Sioux tribe?
A. Richard Harris.

Q. The line, "Remember that night in Montana when we said there'd be no room for doubt," is from what Jimmy Buffet song?
A. "Come Monday".

Entertainment Word Search

```
B I U W O D T Q D L F T Q K K S U Z H C Y H Z T C D Q B
W K M N N F H O D F N X L S L F Y U Y U M A L T Z A C B
H Q Y B D R E R E Y V X P E A S E F G P E M P C L L Q O
F U R B R Y A I N X W Z V O E Y Y L D W R B M P E T B D
P I N N U G T F N I B Q U R L C H C C F K U E J J O X W
I W A E M X E M I O J E W E B X A V U N J R L V N N A O
C Q L W M H A J S H N I W H W O M A I I M G G V O G L Z
N A O O O C M F Q D N I K T Q B C Y T A Q E I M R A U G
P G Y Y N H R R U K S Y Y S O Q X F X C M R B B T N O F
C W X R D H I Y A A G B Y O P F Z I M C W L S N H G S L
E T W R Y M J F I G H D N M R R V Z L O Q D O N F T S Y
E K T A Y F F Y D S S K D L M A U C N R A V N E O G I F
C R B G M T G F A C F Q J A P N Z Y V D T S U W R S M I
N K A F K O L A R S E B J N T K A T N I S J I S K A F S
A J W A O O M E N Z J L P O G Z Z U W O T F K C G H O H
L G R E S R A G K L R Y U O Z A Q Z K N R V U A R I I I
A L Y U O R L X W A W C I U A P E U D N O F G S V Z V N
V L S N K E T N E Z H H X X D P U B I D W J T T W Z G G
Y I M Q V T J P W A H T I S Z A T M Q M M U G E U D W C
T K U T J T I R B O B K Z T D W Y H B F H C T R W N J L
R D Q D B I X L K G T Y Y J E L F R G A D X Z W B M Y R
E A E O C B E C U R S S F H V F K O M L R L U A W X F O
B O C E J S T Z R N I A I P Q U I G P A O T T E W M U X
I R N A Y R G E M B R V Z W P D M S M C U X W X N W N Q
L Z M Z G W E W V I W P A K E J B O H V S H C P V F S J
O Q L I N W Z N B E G X D C S L G I M V U V P K G D E C
O T A T P S B B X F H I S J D N H O R W A V T B Y A O S
M D X H H G Z B X S J H C N I P F X I Z F V V N V J L S
```

Myrna Loy	Dalton gang	Northfork	Untouchables	roadkill
Norma Ashby	hamburger	Garryowen	Bitterroot	Whitefish
The A Team	Liberty Valance	Mel Gibson	Meg Ryan	Dennis Quaid
newscaster	Almost Heroes	Huey Lewis	Frank Zappa	Pearl Jam
fondue	flyfishing	Drummond	Ingomar	accordion
Lewistown	Missoula			

Answers on page 154

Geography Crossword

Science & Nature Scramble

1. ETERPUMTR ANSSW — trumpeter swans
2. ATLYL EKAL — Tally Lake
3. LSSNRDEEWI — wilderness
4. CEAIRGL — Glacier
5. RBYEEELK TPI — Berkeley Pit
6. LAIURNBCSO — binoculars
7. AMCSA — Camas
8. ETDLHAAF LAEK — Flathead Lake
9. PRIAIER ODG — Prairie dog
10. SONIB — bison
11. HIBRNOG EPSHE — bighorn sheep
12. GUALCTRERUI — Agriculture
13. GVONLINTIS — Livingston
14. EIAMPG — magpie
15. REIYDSEB — Birdseye
16. PHSIPEAR — sapphire
17. EENTOSYLWLO — Yellowstone
18. NOSRIUDA — dinosaur
19. COHNOKI — Chinook
20. SHDFPAILED — Paddlefish
21. ELOATPEN — antelope
22. GRLYIZZ — Grizzly

History Word Search

Art & Literature Word Scramble

1. YDUR IOUTA — Rudy Autio
2. RHCLAEI ERLUSSL — Charlie Russell
3. GNAIVIIR TCIY — Virginia City
4. RLDAFIGE YNTUCO — Garfield County
5. ORYHODT OJSNHON — Dorothy Johnson
6. ELEVYN MNOEACR — Evelyn Cameron
7. OBB RCRIVES — Bob Scriver
8. YRBEKELE IPT — Berkeley Pit
9. RIITSP LWOF — Spirit Wolf
10. OVNESILOILP — Poisonville
11. HTE ATSL ESTB ALECP — The Last Best Place
12. RIOPHCTAGP EAVC STETA AKPR — Pictograph Cave State Park
13. EQMAOU ITSKUM — Moquea Stumik
14. YAWLL CEMAR — Wally McRae
15. TYOALR DNGROO — Taylor Gordon
16. OFOLS WCOR — Fools Crow
17. AMEL REDE — Lame Deer
18. MOETN LDOAK — Monte Dolak
19. AGEDR PAXNO — Edgar Paxon
20. OANMRN MCELAAN — Norman Maclean

Sports & Leisure Crossword

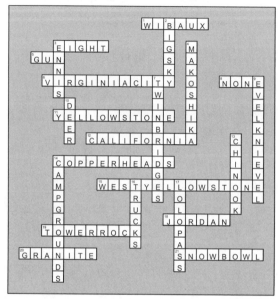

Entertainment Word Search

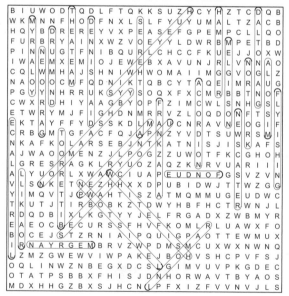

Q. WHO HAS GREAT BOOKS ON MONTANA?
A. RIVERBEND PUBLISHING

A few Montana favorites....

Copper Camp: The Lusty Story of Butte, Montana
The Writers Project of Montana
The people's story of the richest hill on earth during its wild and wide-open heyday. A rollicking Montana classic.

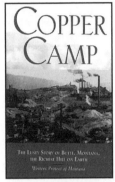

Great Montana Bear Stories
Ben Long
This book educates about living in bear country as it entertains with true stories about grizzly bears and black bears.

The Man Who Shot Liberty Valance
Dorothy M. Johnson
By the finest writer of western stories in the 20th century. Includes "A Man Called Horse," "The Hanging Tree," and "Lost Sister."

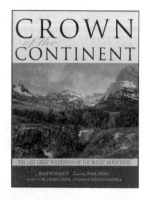
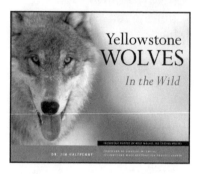
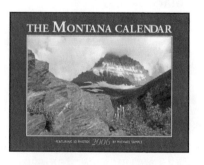